CHILDREN'S WORLD
ATLAS

CHILDREN'S WORLD
ATLAS

Written by
John Farndon

www.alligatorbooks.co.uk

CHILDREN'S WORLD ATLAS

© 2007 Alligator Books Limited

Published by
Alligator Books Limited
Gadd House, Arcadia Avenue
London N3 2JU

Printed in Malaysia

Contents

NORTH
AMERICA

*PACIFIC
OCEAN*

ARCTIC OCEAN

Arctic Circle

EUROPE

ASIA

ANTIC

EAN

f Cancer

AFRICA

*PACIFIC
OCEAN*

Equator

UTH

ERICA

*INDIAN
OCEAN*

Tropic of Capricorn

AUSTRALIA

Antarctic Circle

ANTARCTICA

Using this Atlas

The *Children's World Atlas* can be used either as a reference book to find out essential facts about the world, or as a treasure trove of fascinating insights into countries and the way people live.

The essential facts are mostly contained in the detailed **Face the facts** section above the maps. Here you will find the vital statistics, such as highest mountain, capital, population, natural resources and so on.

On the maps, you will see a range of **icons,** each with its own caption telling you important things that, together, give you an idea of what characterizes the country or region.

At the bottom of the page you can find out more about **the people of the country or region and their way of life.**

The maps in this atlas are arranged in four continental groups: the Americas – North and South America; Europe; Asia and Africa. Each group is introduced by a continental map. Within the four groups, the maps show either countries or regions. Australia, New Zealand, the Arctic and Antarctica follow at the end of the atlas after the Africa maps.

Capital cities
○ OSLO
A yellow circle next to a place name means it is a capital city.

Finding a place
Place names on the maps are listed in alphabetical order in the index, pages 76-80. After each place name you'll find a page number and a grid reference such as 52 H14. Turn to page 52. Find H on the top or bottom border of the map. Find 14 on the left or right border. Trace an imaginary line across the map from the H and from the 14. The place in question – Samarkand – will be close to where they meet.

Figures
To save space and give the maximum information, we have used our own particular way of writing figures. Figures above one million are always written as 1 m(million), 1.2 m, 5 m and so on. The letter m also means metres, when we give measurements.

Highest mountains, longest rivers
For every map, we name the highest peak within the area of the map. We have also named a selection of the other high peaks. For the longest river, we give the entire length of the river from source to mouth, even if it flows through several countries not on the featured map.

Left, the Taj Mahal - see page 56.

Where on Earth?

North pole

Prime meridian

Equator

Finding somewhere on Earth is made simple by the system of criss-cross grids called latitude and longitude. Lines of latitude are imaginary circles drawn around the Earth parallel to the equator, which is why they are called parallels. Lines of longitude are imaginary circles (proper name, meridians) drawn right round the world through the poles, dividing the world into segments like those of an orange.

Both latitude and longitude are measured in degrees as if taken from the centre of the Earth. Figures for latitude are given in degrees north or south of the equator. So, the equator has a latitude of 0° and the North Pole has a latitude of 90°N (North). Figures for longitude are given in degrees west or east of the Prime Meridian, the meridian running through Greenwich in London.

Flattening the globe

The round world is shown on flat maps by using map projections. It's as if light is shone through the globe to project on to paper the criss-crossing grid of longitude and latitude lines. Everything can be located in its right place on the grid. In practice, the projections are made mathematically rather than with light, but the principle is the same. There are scores of different methods of projection, but each is a compromise, showing some features accurately while others are distorted.

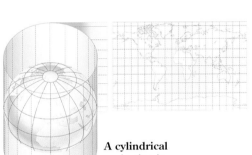

A cylindrical projection is made as if light is shone from the centre of the globe on to a surrounding cylinder of paper which is then rolled out flat. This shows all the Earth on a single map, but exaggerates the size of land (and sea) towards the poles.

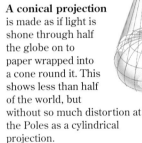

A conical projection is made as if light is shone through half the globe on to paper wrapped into a cone round it. This shows less than half of the world, but without so much distortion at the Poles as a cylindrical projection.

A planar or azimuthal projection is made as if light is shone through half the globe on to a flat piece of paper. These are usually circular maps showing only half the world at a time. Features around the outside are exaggerated in size.

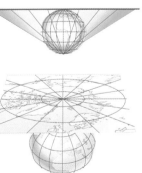

The Mercator projection This is the most widely used projection, a type of cylindrical projection made mathematically by plotting lines of latitude so that the distance between them increases as the lines move farther away from the equator. It is named after the Dutch map-maker Gerardus Mercator (1512–94), who thought of it. The maps in this atlas are mostly cylindrical or conical projections, and include some Mercator, or Mercator-like projections.

Making maps

Ground surveys
In the past, most maps were made by surveys of the ground. Surveyors would painstakingly measure out the land using simple geometrical principles such as triangulation. With triangulation, a surveyor measures a 'baseline' between two fixed points. He then uses an instrument called a theodolite to find the angle of sight lines to a distant point from each end of the baseline. This point completes a triangle. Knowing the baseline and the angle of the two sightlines pinpoints the distance of the point without actually measuring it.

Aerial surveys
From the 1930s on, more and more maps were made, or at least updated, using aerial surveys – that is, photographs from aircraft. The aircraft flies over the survey area taking overlapping pairs of pictures. Each picture of a pair gives a slightly different view of the ground, like each of our eyes. When the two are viewed through a device called a stereoscope, it gives a 3-D image which enables cartographers to work out heights.

Satellite imagery
In the last 30 years, our view of the world has been revolutionized by satellites in space. Spacecraft gave us the first photographic evidence that the Earth is a globe. There are now scores of different satellites circling the Earth. Some simply take photographs. (The maps in this atlas were made with the help of satellite photographs.) Others respond to particular wavebands of radiation, such as infrared or single colours, to show different features of the earth's surface – such as areas of healthy vegetation, broadleaved forests, ocean currents, clouds, ocean surface temperatures and much, much more.

Satellite pinpoints
Satellites have not only given us new and revealing images of the Earth's surface. They have also revolutionized the ease and accuracy with which we can pinpoint things on the ground. Satellite laser ranging (SLR) involves bouncing a laser beam off a satellite between two ground stations, and enables millimetre shifts of continents thousands of kilometres apart to be measured.

Planet Earth

The Earth is a very small place. It is just one of the smaller planets of the nine that make up the solar system – the collection of globes and space debris that circle the Sun, our local star. The Sun, in turn, is just a medium-sized star among the millions on one of the arms of the vast spiralling galaxy of stars called the Milky Way, one of the billions of galaxies in the Universe.

Pluto
Neptune
Uranus

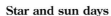
Earth
Venus
Mercury
Mars
Jupiter
Saturn

The nine planets of the Solar System
Distances between them are much greater than they appear in this artistic impression, but their relative sizes are as shown.

Day and night
At any one time, half the world is facing the Sun and is brightly lit; the other half is facing away and is in darkness. We get day and night as the Earth spins us towards the Sun and away again. Because the Earth is turning eastwards, the Sun comes up in the east and sinks again in the west. The Earth turns round once every 24 hours, which is why Earth days are 24 hours long.

Seasons
The Earth's axis is not quite at a right angle to the Sun, but tilted over at an angle of 23.5°, and this is why we have seasons. As the Earth journeys around the Sun, the tilt swings different parts of the world to face the Sun more directly than others.

Star and sun days
In fact, there are two ways of measuring a day: by the Sun (solar day) and by the distant stars (sidereal day). A sidereal day is the time it takes for the Earth to turn right round until the stars are in exactly the same place in the sky again, which is 23 hours 56 mins and 4.09 secs. A solar day, at 24 hours exactly, is slightly longer because the Earth moves a little way round the Sun during the course of a day. So it has to turn 1° further before the Sun is back in the same place in the sky.

Turn of speed
The world may seem perfectly still, but it is moving through space all the time, faster than you can imagine. It is not only spinning on its axis like a top at over 1600 km/h – faster than most jet planes. It is also hurtling around the Sun at over 100,000 km/h. Even so, the journey around the Sun is so long – almost a billion kilometres – that it takes 365 days to complete, which is why our year is 365 days long.

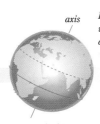

axis

In spring, your part of the world tilts towards the Sun again, bringing longer, warmer days.

In summer, your part of the world tilts towards the Sun. Days are longer, the sun climbs higher in the sky and stays in sight longer. The weather is warm.

In winter, your part of the world is tilted over, away from the sun. The sun is low in the sky, days are short and generally very cold.

In autumn, your part of the world begins to tilt away from the Sun. Days get shorter, and the sun does not climb as high in the sky. Shadows are longer and the weather cooler.

Earth data

Diameter at Equator	12,758 km
Diameter pole to pole	12,712 km
Circumference at the Equator	40,024 km
Distance from the Sun	149.6 million km
Length of orbit round Sun	939,886,400 km
Time taken to orbit Sun	365.242 days
Time taken to spin round once	23 hours 56 minutes
Tilt of axis in space	23.5°
Speed through space	105,000 km/h

The shape of the Earth
The Earth is a not perfect sphere. Because it spins faster at the equator than at the poles, it is shaped more like a tangerine, bulging slightly at the equator and flattened at the poles. Scientists used to say it was an oblate spheroid (flattened ball). Now satellite measurements have shown that there are slight irregularities, so they simply describe it as geoid, which means Earth-shaped.

Leap years
The Earth takes 365.242 days to go round the Sun once, not 365. As it would be awkward to have 365.242 days in a year, the Western calendar adds an extra day every fourth year, called a leap year, but misses one leap year per century for three centuries out of four. This way, our calendar is nearly always in step with the Earth's progress through space, and the Earth is in the same place relative to the Sun on each day of the year.

Inside the Earth

The Earth is not just a solid ball. Earthquake waves and vibrations from explosions have showed that it is actually a complex structure. Around the outside is a thin shell of rock called the crust, just 40 km thick on average beneath the continents and less than 6 km thick beneath the oceans. Beneath the crust is a thick mantle of rock or 'magma' so hot that it flows like treacle (only very, very slowly). More than 2890 km below the surface there is a core of metal. The outer core is so hot, it is always molten; the inner core is solid because pressures here are so great that it cannot melt, even though temperatures reach 7000°C.

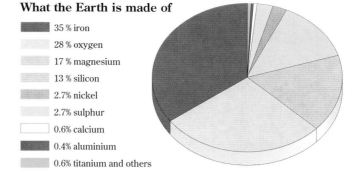

What the Earth is made of

- 35 % iron
- 28 % oxygen
- 17 % magnesium
- 13 % silicon
- 2.7% nickel
- 2.7% sulphur
- 0.6% calcium
- 0.4% aluminium
- 0.6% titanium and others

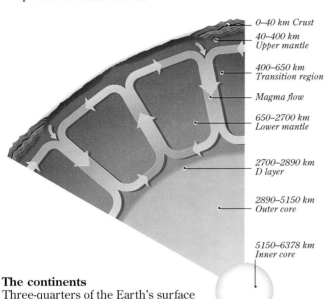

- 0–40 km Crust
- 40–400 km Upper mantle
- 400–650 km Transition region
- Magma flow
- 650–2700 km Lower mantle
- 2700–2890 km D layer
- 2890–5150 km Outer core
- 5150–6378 km Inner core

Rock and iron

At least 80 different chemical elements are found naturally on the Earth, but it is really a planet of rock and iron.
- The crust is mainly quartz – silicon dioxide – and other silicates such as feldspar.
- The upper mantle is mostly olivine and pyroxene – iron and magnesium silicates.
- The lower mantle is mostly silicon, magnesium and oxygen.
- The core is mostly iron, with a little nickel.

How did the Earth begin?

The Earth is about 4.6 billion years old and formed from a vast cloud of hot gas and dust whirling round the newly formed Sun. It probably began when tiny pieces of space debris within the cloud, called planetesimals, began to bunch together under the influence of their gravity. It was entirely molten at first, and dense material such as iron and nickel sank to the centre while lighter material such as silicon floated to the top. Very soon, the Earth began to cool and a crust began to form on the outside.

The continents

Three-quarters of the Earth's surface is covered by water. Most of the land is in seven huge chunks called continents – North and South America, Europe, Asia, Africa, Australia and Antarctica. Rocks in the heart of these continents are very ancient – at least 3.8 billion years – but the continents have not stayed in the same place. In fact, they are drifting very slowly around the globe all the time. Indeed 220 million years ago, the continents were joined together in a giant supercontinent called Pangea, but 200 million years ago it began to break up, and its fragments form the continents we know today.

Rigid plates

The boundary between the crust and the mantle is called the Mohorovicic discontinuity. But the underside of the crust and upper mantle are in some ways so alike that they blend together. Geologists often refer to the lithosphere, extending 100 km below the surface, and the asthenosphere, going down a further 300 km.

Tectonic plates

The Earth's rigid shell is cracked into eight large pieces and perhaps two dozen smaller pieces. These pieces are called tectonic plates. As they move slowly around, they carry the continents with them. They also set off earthquakes as they grind together, and throw up mountains where they collide – and play a major part in bringing molten material from the earth's interior to the surface in volcanoes.

Time zones

As the Earth spins round, the Sun is always rising in one place and setting in another: the time of day varies all round the world. So the world is divided into 24 time zones, one for each hour of the day. As you go east around the world, you put clocks forward by one hour for each zone – until you reach a line running through the Pacific called the International Date Line. If you carry on past the Date Line, you carry on putting the clock forward, but put the calendar one day back.

Each time zone is about 15 degrees of longitude.

The time at 0 degrees longitude is called Greenwich Mean Time.

Time zones are not always regular bands, but may bend according to national boundaries.

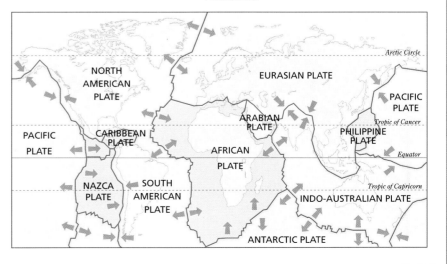

Air and oceans

Earth is a very watery planet, and much of its surface is submerged under five great oceans – the Pacific, the Atlantic, the Indian, the Southern (around Antarctica) and the Arctic. Only a quarter is land. Wrapped around it all is a thin, transparent cocoon of gases called the atmosphere. Without the atmosphere, the Earth would be as lifeless as the Moon. The atmosphere gives us the air we need to breathe; it provides us with a supply of clean water to drink; it protects us from the sun's harmful rays and it traps its warmth.

Ocean currents

The water in the oceans is always on the move. Winds whip the surface into waves and generate surface currents – giant rivers in the sea that flow for thousands of kilometres from one side of the ocean to the other. There are also deep currents created as the combination of the sun's warmth and chemical differences in the water stir up the oceans.

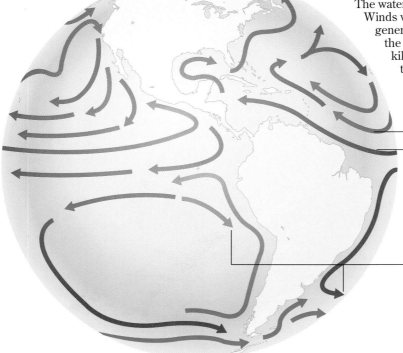

The surface currents (warm – red, and cold – blue) are split either side of the equator into huge rings called gyres that circulate continually round the margins of each ocean. In the northern hemisphere gyres circulate clockwise; in the south, they circulate anticlockwise. Branching off from the gyres are many eddies and swirls.

The direction of surface currents depends on both the winds blowing over the oceans and the effect of the Earth's rotation.

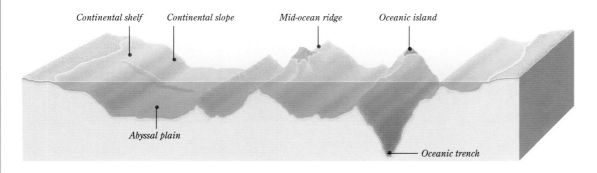

Continental shelf   *Continental slope*   *Mid-ocean ridge*   *Oceanic island*

Abyssal plain

Oceanic trench

The ocean bed

Until recently, we knew very little about the ocean depths. But oceanographic surveys and voyages in submersibles (special diving craft), sometimes to amazing depths, have revealed an undersea landscape as varied as the continents, complete with mountains, valleys and plains.

The continental shelf is a narrow band of shallow water rarely more than 130 m deep around the edge of the continents.

The continental slope is a steep descent from the continental shelf to the deep ocean.

Much of the ocean basin bed is a flat plain, called the abyssal plain, 2000 m below the surface and covered with a thick slime called ooze.

Fresh water

Less than 1 per cent of the water on Earth is fresh, but this small supply is never used up, going round and round in an endless cycle. The water cycle begins as water is evaporated by the sun from oceans and lakes and is given out from plants. This water vapour drifts up through the atmosphere, then as the air cools, it condenses into droplets of water or ice crystals, forming clouds. Water falls from clouds as rain or snow, which either soaks into the ground and is taken up by plants, or runs off in rivers, eventually finding its way into lakes or oceans.

Layers in the air

Scientists divide the atmosphere into layers. We live in the bottom layer, called the troposphere. This layer gets its warmth from the ground, which is heated by visible light from the sun. So temperatures in this layer get steadily lower as you go higher away from the ground. But above 12 km up, in the stratosphere, temperatures actually begin to rise as you climb higher. The ozone gas in the stratosphere heats up by directly absorbing the sun's ultraviolet light. Higher still, the mesosphere is heated as oxygen and nitrogen are warmed by extreme ultraviolet light – but temperatures begin to drop with height as the gases get thinner and thinner. In the thermosphere above, they are thinner still, but because they are exposed to the full glare of the sun, temperatures soar to 2000°C.

Earth's special atmosphere

Earth is the only planet in the solar system that has plentiful oxygen. This is because plants put it there billions of years ago – and keep it there today – as they draw carbon dioxide from the air to provide food, and release oxygen in return in a sunlight-driven process called photosynthesis. The nitrogen and other gases mix with the oxygen, but only rarely chemically combine, leaving it free for us to breathe.

Nitrogen 78 per cent
Oxygen 21 per cent
Argon 0.93 per cent
Carbon dioxide 0.03 per cent
Neon, helium, and other gases 0.04 per cent

Letting the sun in

In the stratosphere, there is a small amount of the gas ozone, creating what is called the ozone layer. This vital layer shields us from lethal ultraviolet rays from the sun. But it is being attacked by man-made gases such as CFCs (chlorofluorocarbons) once used in aerosol sprays and as coolants in refrigerators. Now holes in the ozone appear over the South and North Poles every spring and are lasting longer each year, despite bans on CFCs.

The troposphere contains almost 75 per cent of the atmosphere's gases. It gets colder as you go higher until you reach the tropopause (the top of the troposphere) about 12 km up.

The mesosphere is too thin in gases to absorb much heat, so it gets colder with height, plunging to −120°C at the mesopause (the top of the mesosphere), 80 km above the ground.

The thermosphere is even thinner than the mesosphere but is heated by ultraviolet rays from the sun to over 2000°C at the top, about 300 km above the ground.

The stratosphere extends from about 12 km to 50 km above the ground and contains 19 per cent of the atmosphere's gases. It gets warmer as you go higher, from −60°C to about 10°C at the stratopause (the top of the stratosphere).

The exosphere is the outermost layer of the atmosphere, extending to more than 700 km above the ground. Gases here are very rarefied – that is, they are very rare – as the atmosphere fades away into space.

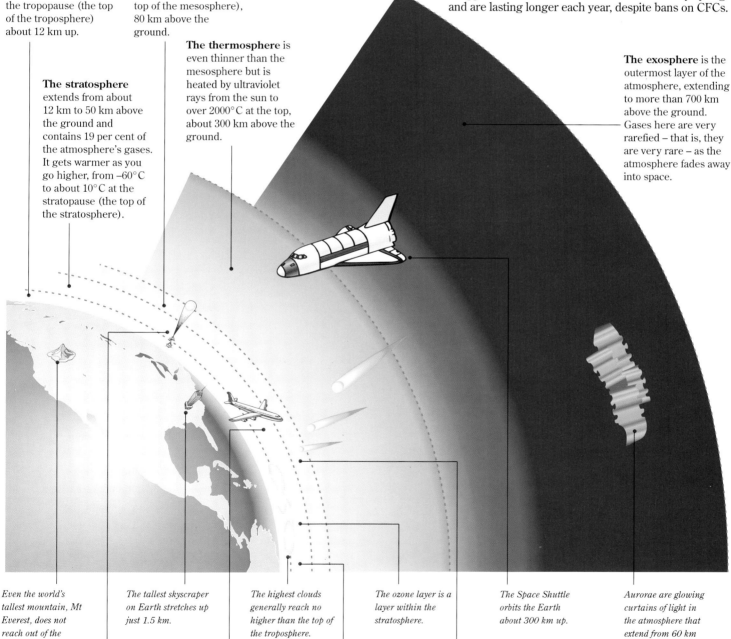

Even the world's tallest mountain, Mt Everest, does not reach out of the troposphere.

The tallest skyscraper on Earth stretches up just 1.5 km.

The highest clouds generally reach no higher than the top of the troposphere.

The ozone layer is a layer within the stratosphere.

The Space Shuttle orbits the Earth about 300 km up.

Aurorae are glowing curtains of light in the atmosphere that extend from 60 km above the ground to over 700 km.

Weather balloons float right up into the stratosphere.

Jetliners fly at over 12 km, in the calm, clear air of the stratosphere.

The only clouds in the stratosphere are very rare 'nacreous' clouds at 22–24 km.

Meteors burn up in the mesosphere.

The living world

Earth is the only place in the solar system – perhaps in the entire universe – where life thrives. Earth is uniquely fitted for life because it has an atmosphere of gas, has water on the surface, and is neither too hot like Venus nor too cold like the outer planets. But even on Earth, life is confined to a narrow zone between the lower layers of the atmosphere and the ocean bed. Within this narrow zone, however, there is an astonishing variety of life.

Tropical rainforest
Heavy rain and high temperatures make tropical rainforests the richest of all plant and animal habitats. They are home to 40 per cent of all plant and animal species – a single hectare may have a hundred kinds of tree. Despite its richness, tropical rainforest is fragile, because all the nutrients are tied up in the trees rather than the soil as they are in many other biomes.

Life support systems

The total package of the world's living things is called the biosphere – plants, animals and everything. It is not separate from the non-living world, but linked intimately with it – with soils, rocks, air and water. The biosphere is divided into dozens of different geographical regions or 'biomes' around the world. Within each biome, there are many different ecosystems, which are communities of living things all interacting together and with their surroundings. Within each ecosystem, each plant or creature has its own particular habitat – its preferred place to live.

Climate and biome

Biomes are essentially related to climate and the vegetation it creates – desert, tropical rainforest, grassland and so on. But they can also be linked to particular kinds of environment, such as the ocean or mountains or wetlands. Each has its own particular range of animals and plants.

How life began

Life probably began about 3.8 billion years ago. For some time, the early Earth was a seething mass of volcanoes and smoke and the early oceans were probably acidic. Experiments have shown that, even in such a hostile environment, a spark of lightning can join chemicals together to form amino acids, the basic chemicals of life. But no one knows how amino acids joined up to become the first life forms. All we do know is that they probably appeared in the oceans first, and they are likely to have been single-celled, microscopic bacteria called *Archaebacteria*, which now live in similarly hostile conditions in volcanic openings under the sea and feed on chemicals.

Arctic Circle

Tropic of Cancer

Equator

Tropic of Capricorn

Very soon after the creation of the first microscopic bacteria (*see* How life began, *above*), another kind of bacteria called blue-green algae appeared. They used sunlight to help them draw carbon dioxide from the air, and as they did, they gave the air oxygen. Bacteria are 'prokaryotes' – that is, living cells with no complex structures or a central nucleus. The first 'eukaryotes', living cells with a nucleus, were large single-celled microbes such as amoebas.

The first proper animals, such as sponges and jellyfish, made from hundreds of cells, appeared 700 million years ago.

About 600 million years ago, creatures with hard parts such as shells and bones appeared.

About 400 million years ago, fish, the first creatures with backbones, appeared.

About 400 million years ago, life appeared on land as plants and insects began to thrive.

About 350 million years ago, amphibians began to emerge from the water to become the first land animals with backbones. All land animals evolved from these creatures.

Hot desert

Arid and semi-arid lands cover over 30 per cent of the Earth's land surface. Despite lack of water and high temperatures in the hot deserts, very few are actually completely devoid of life. But the creatures who live here must be specially adapted to the conditions or be very hardy, like insects.

Savannah or tropical grassland

This covers 20 per cent of the world's land surface. They are dominated by grasses and sedges, but may have large open woods and clumps of bushes and trees and water holes. They are often roamed by huge herds of grazing animals such as zebras and antelopes.

Temperate grassland

Temperate grasslands are grasslands in the mid-latitudes where winters are cool and summers are warm. The three main areas of temperate grassland are the steppes of Russia and Asia, the prairies of the USA and the pampas of Uruguay.

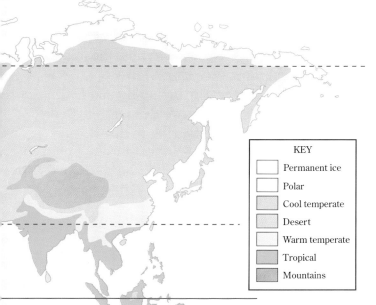

KEY

☐ Permanent ice
☐ Polar
☐ Cool temperate
☐ Desert
☐ Warm temperate
☐ Tropical
☐ Mountains

Temperate forest

In the cold north of Asia and North America are boreal forests or taiga dominated by conifer trees such as pine and spruce. Nearer the tropics are broadleaved evergreen forests with trees such as holm oaks and magnolia. In between are deciduous forests, where trees such as oak, beech and hickory lose their leaves in winter in order to save water.

Tundra

The tundra is the cold, treeless region in places such as northern Siberia, northern Canada and Alaska. Temperatures here are less than −10°C for at least half the year, so vegetation is limited to mosses, lichens and sedges. But a number of creatures adapted to the cold survive here, such as the polar bear.

Mountain

The cold stops most vegetation growing on mountain peaks, giving them a tundra-like biome, but trees and plants may thrive lower down, below the 'tree line' which is higher the nearer you get to the equator.

From **220 million years ago to 65 million years ago,** *the Earth was dominated by giant reptiles called dinosaurs.*

65 million years ago, *the dinosaurs all died out – perhaps after a giant asteroid hit the Earth, filling the air with so much dust that it blocked out the sun.*

With the death of the dinosaurs, mammals and birds began to spread.

About **20 million years ago,** *vast grasslands encouraged the rise of large hooved animals such as horses, as well as cats and dogs.*

The first human-like creatures or 'hominids' appeared about **4 million years ago.**

In the Ice Ages, **2 million to 10,000 years ago,** *creatures with thick coats such as woolly rhinos and mammoths (large hairy, elephant-like creatures) thrived along with giant cave bears and lions which sought shelter from the cold in caves.*

Humans like us (Homo sapiens sapiens) emerged only **about 10,000 years ago.**

A world of rich and poor

Manhattan's skyline, prior to the 11 September 2001 terrorist attacks which destroyed the World Trade Center's twin towers.

There are nearly six billion people in the world, and the population is growing at the rate of one million people every week. Some areas, such as Europe and Southeast Asia, are densely populated. Others are almost empty, for example Siberia and the Sahara desert. In the past, most people lived in the countryside and grew their own food. Now people are, increasingly, moving into cities. Not all of these people have equally easy lives. In Europe, North America, Japan and Australia, many people are poor, but most people live fairly comfortably. But in the rest of the world, including all of Africa and Latin America, most people are desperately poor, and some are starving to death.

North and South

Nearly all the rich nations are in the northern hemisphere, so economists talk of the North–South divide when talking about poverty. The North includes North America, Europe, Japan, Australia and New Zealand, even though the last two are actually in the south. Nearly everyone in the South is poor, but over one billion live in 'absolute poverty'. It is hard to imagine what absolute poverty is, but all these people live in desperate situations. They have no real income and no home. In cities, they sleep rough or in makeshift shacks with no water. They never have enough to eat or drink. They are prone to disease. The children die young. In Zambia, for instance, a child is 20 times more likely to die before the age of ten than in Germany. 450 million people – one person in 12 – are starving or badly nourished, and millions die each year from lack of food or diseases brought on by lack of food.

The widening gap

Sadly, the gap between rich and poor is growing, not shrinking. According to the United Nations, just 358 rich people have as much money as all the poorest 2.3 billion combined. Signs of the poverty gap are visible in many ways, but one way economists look at it is in terms of Gross National Product (GNP) per person – that is, what each person would get if a country's entire income was divided equally among the population. On this basis, people in the USA earn $31,910 a year and people in Switzerland $38,380 – while people in Mali earn less than $240. The GNP per person in the North is steadily increasing, but in many of the poorer countries, it is actually decreasing. So the North, with less than a quarter of the people, has more than three-quarters of the money.

Does industry work?

Many economists insist that the North is rich because of its industry. So countries in the South have been encouraged to borrow money to develop their own industry. But attempts to build industries here have often failed to lift people out of poverty – and sometimes done the reverse. Many people move to growing cities, for example São Paulo or Mexico City, only to find more hardship than in the country. The drive to industrialize quickly means factories are often dangerous to work in and pollute the environment.

In debt

In the 1970s, many countries in the South were persuaded to borrow huge amounts of money to get industry going. But even paying the interest on these loans is now costing them a fortune, often more than their entire income. In the late 1990s, to help poorer countries, several industrialized nations have rescheduled or even cancelled debt payments.

Raising livestock

There are now two-and-a-half times as many farm animals in the world as there are humans – more than 14 billion all told. All these animals need an area three times as large as the USA on which to graze. Farm animals such as cows, sheep and goats can feed on grass and other plants inedible to humans, so they can be reared in many places where crops will not grow – on damp meadows, arid grasslands and high mountain slopes. But in many places they are raised on good 'cropland', and they are fed coming up to half of the world's entire cereal crop. In the USA, farm animals eat three-quarters of the grain harvest.

Cash crops

Many farmers in the South grow food just for themselves and their families. But the richness of the North has encouraged well-off farmers to take most of the best land to grow crops to sell to the North for money, rather than growing food for local people. These crops, called 'cash crops', include everything from sugar and bananas to coffee and tea, and many people in the South, especially in Latin America, work for low wages on plantations growing cash crops. Wheat can also be a cash crop. India grows huge amounts of wheat – yet many people here are malnourished, because they cannot afford the prices wheat fetches on export markets.

Growing crops

Plants provide most of the world with its 'staple' (basic) food, whether it is bread or soya, and an area one and a half times as big as the USA is devoted to growing crops. Cereals such as wheat, rice, maize, barley, oats and rye are the world's major sources of food. The choice of crop depends mostly on climate and soil, but also on the style of farming. Cassava, for instance, is not suited to highly mechanized farming, but grows well in dry places, which is why it is grown widely in Africa. Wheat is grown all over the world, but Europe is the world's leading grower of potatoes, barley and rye, while Asia grows 90 per cent of its rice and sweet potatoes as well as huge amounts of beans and sorghum. The USA grows almost half the world's maize.

Energy

The modern world consumes huge amounts of energy, providing everything from light and warmth to power for cars and machines. Over 99 per cent comes ultimately from the sun, but we use very little of it directly. Instead, most energy comes from fossil fuels – coal, oil and natural gas – created by plants which absorbed sunlight long ago. Fossil fuels would take many millions of years to replace, so they are called non-renewable. Renewable sources such as trees, running water and wind give us less than 5 per cent of our energy. The world is using 100 times as much energy as it did a century ago, and the amount is rising steadily – so there is serious concern that eventually fossil fuels will run out. Discoveries of huge new reserves around the Caspian Sea have merely delayed the crisis.

Balance of trade

Countries trade with each other in order to buy food and things that they can't make themselves. Some people favour 'free trade' which means that there are no restrictions at all on the goods and services that are traded. Others believe that controls such as taxes on foreign goods (called tariffs) are essential for protecting home industries from foreign rivals. Most countries use a mixture of the two. Countries measure their success in terms of 'balance of payments'. This is the difference between the amount they sell abroad (exports) and the amount they buy (imports).

The Americas

The Americas stretch over 15,000 km almost from Pole to Pole. The far southern tip of South America is the most southerly point of land outside Antarctica, while northern reaches of North America extend far inside the Arctic Circle. In between, there is a vast range of landscapes, from the huge steamy rainforests of the Amazon to the bleak tundra of northern Canada. There is an equally vast range of countries and lifestyles.

North America is dominated by the United States of America. This was colonized by the people now called Native Americans over 11,000 years ago, as they migrated from Asia across the Bering Straits in the far north. But European settlers arrived here in the 17th century, and gradually pushed westwards, driving the Native Americans out of the way, and creating a huge new country, which now has a population of over 250 million.

With a wealth of natural resources and a large, energetic population, the USA has dominated the world economy since the end of World War II. For a while in the 1950s and 1960s, the USA cornered more than a quarter of the world market in manufactured goods, and Americans earned more money, ate more food, used more energy and drove more cars than anyone else in the world. By the 1980s, though, America had lost ground to rising economies such as Japan, Germany and Korea. The USA regained some of its confidence in the early 1990s, only to suffer another setback with the suicide attacks on New York City and Washington DC on 11 September 2001.

Miles 0 200 400 600 800 1000 1200

Kilometres 0 600 1200 1800

Map labels

Baffin Bay

Davis Strait

Newfoundland

Ellesmere Island

Baffin Island

Hudson Bay

Laurentian Plateau

ARCTIC OCEAN

Beaufort Sea

Great Bear Lake

Mackenzie

Great Slave Lake

Back

Lake Winnipeg

CANADA

Great Plains

Calgary

Winnipeg

Minneapolis

L. Superior

THE GREAT LAKES

L. Michigan L. Huron

L. Ontario

L. Erie

OTTAWA

Quebec

Montreal

Toronto

Detroit

Chicago

Boston

New York

Philadelphia

WASHINGTON DC

St Louis

Missouri

Mississippi

ROCKY MOUNTAINS

UNITED STATES OF

Columbia

Vancouver

Mt. Rainier △

Portland

San Francisco

Yukon

BROOKS RANGE

ALASKA

Mt. McKinley △

Gulf of Alaska

Bering Sea

Bering Strait

ALEUTIAN ISLANDS

Arctic circle

A

OCEAN

Recife
Salvador
Belo Horizonte
Rio de Janeiro
Pôrto Alegre
MONTEVIDEO
Belém
BRAZILIAN HIGHLANDS
São Francisco
BRASÍLIA
Xingu
Amazon
Amazon Basin
Madeira
B R A Z I L
São Paulo
Paraná
PARAGUAY
URUGUAY
BUENOS AIRES
Córdoba
Asunción
CHILE
BOLIVIA
LA PAZ
PERU
Paraguay
Tropic of Capricorn
Santiago
Aconcagua
A R G E N T I N A
Patagonia
Pampas
A N D E S
FALKLAND ISLANDS
(to UK)
Cape Horn

A T L A N T I C
TRINIDAD & TOBAGO
GUYANA
SURINAME
FRENCH GUIANA
GUIANA HIGHLANDS
CARACAS
VENEZUELA
Orinoco
Negro
COLOMBIA
BOGOTÁ
Medellín
Cali
PANAMA
ECUADOR
GALAPAGOS ISLANDS
Equator
LIMA

L A T I N
BAHAMAS
CUBA
DOMINICAN REPUBLIC
HAITI
JAMAICA
PUERTO RICO
Caribbean Sea
Miami
Gulf of Mexico
BELIZE
HONDURAS
GUATEMALA
EL SALVADOR
NICARAGUA
COSTA RICA
Houston
Monterrey
EASTERN SIERRA MADRE
WESTERN SIERRA MADRE
M E X I C O
Guadalajara
MEXICO CITY
Tropic of Cancer
Orleans
Rande
A M E R I C A

P A C I F I C   O C E A N

Latin America (the South and Centre), by contrast with North America, has not been nearly so successful economically. Europeans came to settle here at much the same time as they did in the North. But the sheer distance from Europe, and the alien feel of the predominantly tropical climate and landscape helped keep numbers more limited. Unlike in the North, many Spanish settlers who came here married the local people, and there are now more of their descendants, the mestizos, than any other ethnic group. The other major groups of people here, as in North America, are black people descended from the Africans brought here as slaves between 1518 and 1850.

South America now has the fastest growing population in the world (proportionally), but most people are poor. In the countryside, much of the land is in vast estates and ranches owned by a rich few. So millions of people have moved to fast-growing cities such as São Paulo and Mexico City where many live in shanty settlements.

The heart of South America is the vast Amazon rainforest. But this rich natural habitat, the richest in the world, with thousands of unique species of plants and animals, is being cut for wood and burned to make way for farms, roads and mines at over 260 sq km a day. In the 1980s alone, nearly half of Brazil's rainforest was destroyed. As a result, the last forest-dwelling Indian tribes are threatened with extinction, along with countless species of plants and animals.

ARCTIC OCEAN
EUROPE
ASIA
PACIFIC OCEAN
ATLANTIC OCEAN
AFRICA
INDIAN OCEAN
AUSTRALIA
NORTH AMERICA
SOUTH AMERICA
PACIFIC OCEAN

Canada and Alaska

Canada is the second largest country in the world, stretching over a third of the way around the globe – from the high Rocky Mountains to the damp, misty coast of Newfoundland and Nova Scotia. The frozen north of the country is well inside the Arctic Circle and most people live in the south along the border with the United States, the world's longest border, stretching over 6000 km. Also included here is Alaska, part of the USA, but separated from it by Canada.

ARCTIC OCEAN

Beaufort Sea
Baffin Bay   GREENLAND
RUSSIA   **ALASKA (to USA)**
Bering Sea
Gulf of Alaska
CANADA
Hudson Bay
UNITED STATES OF AMERICA
PACIFIC OCEAN
Gulf of Mexico
MEXICO
ATLANTIC OCEAN

Big bears

The grizzly or silvertop bear is the world's biggest land carnivore and will catch and eat animals as large as ponies and deer. Most of the time, though, it goes for something smaller: for example it catches salmon leaping upstream. But, like most bears, it doesn't only eat meat. Its thick fur makes the grizzly able to cope with the bitter cold of the Canadian winter. Even so, it finds a snug hole in which to hibernate during the worst of the weather.

Cold oil

Alaska's income comes mainly from oil drilled on the northern coast around Prudhoe Bay, then piped south for 1300 km, right across the state through the Trans-Alaska pipeline to Valdez on the south coast. The extreme cold and long months of darkness in winter make Alaska one of the world's toughest places to drill for oil.

The Canadians

Canada is one of the world's wealthiest countries, and most Canadians have a very comfortable lifestyle. Until recently, most were descendants of British, French or other European settlers, and Native Americans, such as the Inuit and Iroquois, made up less than 2 per cent of the population.

Native Americans

Over much of Canada, Native American peoples such as the Iroquois were driven from their ancestral lands when the European settlers arrived. Totem poles, wooden poles carved by tribes on the Pacific coast, can be seen on reservations in Victoria and Vancouver in British Columbia. The pole tells a family's history, showing which clan they belonged to – eagle, bear, and so on. Many Native Americans are now calling for the return of their ancestral lands.

Going underground

It can get so cold in winter here that as much as possible is kept indoors, even underground. Indeed, in Montreal, there are whole shopping malls built entirely underground to save on heating. The first was opened in Place Ville-Marie in 1962 and has dozens of shops and restaurants, and there are now many others, all linked by tunnels to create Montreal's 'Underground City'.

The Inuit

The Inuit are the natives of Greenland and northern Canada. Many of them still hunt and fish as they have done for thousands of years, but they live in modern houses rather than traditional igloos and skin tents. From 1 April, 1999, the Inuit have had their own self-governing homeland in the Northwest Territories, called Nunavut, meaning 'our land' in the Inuit language.

Chinese Canadians

Chinese people first came to Canada in the 19th century to help build the Canadian Pacific Railroad, and there is now a large Chinese community in Vancouver. Vancouver is the main trading port between Canada and Asia, and as Hong Kong prepared for its return to Chinese control in 1997, many wealthy Hong Kong businessmen bought property here. Now many of them have moved to the city, and made Vancouver one of the biggest centres of Chinese culture outside Asia.

Maple syrup

The leaf of the maple tree is Canada's national symbol, and the sap of the tree, a sweet syrup, is one of Canada's food specialities – although most maple syrup sold in the shops is made artificially. Children in Canada make 'maple taffy' by pouring hot maple syrup on to snow so that it hardens into toffee.

French Canada

In Quebec, 80 per cent of the people are of French origin and speak French as their first language. Montreal is the second-largest French-speaking city in the world after Paris. Many people in Quebec want independence from the rest of Canada.

Canadian Pacific

Completing the Canadian Pacific Railroad all the way across Canada in 1885 was one of the greatest engineering achievements of the 19th century. Climbing high over the Rockies through breathtaking passes, it linked the west to the rest of Canada for the first time. One of the most amazing features of the line through the Rockies is a spiral tunnel which winds round and round to climb almost 1000 m.

St. Lawrence Island
Bering Strait
Arctic Circle
BROOKS RANGE
BEAUFORT SEA
ALASKA (toUSA)   Yukon
Porcupine
Mt. McKinley 6194m   **Fairbanks**
Anchorage
ALEUTIAN ISLANDS
Kodiak Island
Mt. Logan 5951m
GULF OF ALASKA
PACIFIC OCEAN
Whitehorse
Juneau
MCKENZIE MOUNTAINS
Mackenzie
Great Bear
Fort Norm
YUKON TERRITORY
ROCKY MOUNTAINS
Yellowkni
Gr Sl La
Peace
QUEEN CHARLOTTE ISLANDS
BRITISH COLUMBIA
VANCOUVER ISLAND
Edmonton
ALBERT
Banff
Calg
Vancouver
Victoria
UNITE

M   N   O   P   Q   R   S   T   U   V   W

FACE THE FACTS...

❖ The land
The highest peak in Canada is Mt Logan (5951 m). The longest river is the Mackenzie, linked to the Peace by the Great Slave Lake (4241 km).

❖ Climate
Varies considerably. On the whole, long, cold winters, especially in the far north, and relatively short but often hot summers.

❖ Population
There are 30.5 m people

in Canada, mostly around Vancouver and in the southeast.

❖ Capital
Ottawa.

❖ Natural resources
Canada is the world's largest producer of zinc, potash and uranium, second largest of nickel, cadmium, asbestos and sulphur. It is also rich in gold, copper, lead, iron, molybdenum, cobalt, oil, natural gas and coal. There is a massive diamond source in the Northwest Territories.

❖ Farming
Only 7 per cent of Canada is farmed, but this is still a huge area. The prime farm land is the prairies of western Canada – Saskatchewan, Alberta and Manitoba – where there are vast fields of wheat, and beef cattle are raised. Quebec is the world's largest

producer of maple syrup.

❖ Forestry
Almost half of Canada is covered in forests, making 10 per cent of the world's entire forest stock, and the country is the world's largest exporter of forest products. The main area for logging is British Columbia.

❖ Fishing and trapping
Canada has a large fishing industry. Well over 60 m dollars is made from animal pelts each year.

❖ Industry and commerce
Much of Canada's industry is in the so-called Golden Horseshoe around the west of Lake Ontario, where they make cars (General Motors), steel, aircraft and ships, and produce canned fruit. Other major industries include newsprint, pulp, chemicals, aluminium refining, and electronics

goods. Toronto and Montreal are major financial centres. Most people, though, work in service industries such as education.

❖ Government
Canada is a parliamentary democracy with a prime minister. The British Queen, represented by the Governor-General, is the head of state.

❖ Religion
More than 70 per cent of Canadians are Christian.

❖ Currency
Canadian dollar.

❖ Sport
The national game is lacrosse, originally a Native American game. Winter sports such as ice hockey, skiing and skating are popular; also white-water rafting and canoeing.

Ice house
Igloos were originally built as winter homes by the Inuit people, but are now used only for overnight stays on hunts. However, igloo-making is still taught at Inuit schools. Ice blocks are cut and placed so that they spiral up into a dome. The final block is called the icing block or *qulluti* and must fit snugly to give the igloo strength.

The Grand Banks
The Grand Banks off the coast of Newfoundland were once one of the world's best fishing grounds, yielding huge catches of cod. But they have been so overfished that fishing there is now strictly controlled. In 1992, the situation reached a crisis point and commercial fishing for cod in the area was banned altogether.

Ellesmere Island

QUEEN ELIZABETH ISLANDS

aks nd

Victoria Island

Baffin Bay

Baffin Island

Arctic Circle

ATLANTIC OCEAN

NORTHWEST TERRITORIES

Hudson Bay

Lake Athabasca

● Churchill

MANITOBA

Belcher Island

Labrador

NEWFOUNDLAND

C   A   N   A   D   A

KATCHEWAN

Saskatchewan

Lake Winnipeg

ONTARIO

QUEBEC

Newfoundland

St. John's

Cape Race

Gulf of St. Lawrence

PRINCE EDWARD ISLAND

NEW BRUNSWICK

NOVA SCOTIA

○ Saskatoon

○ Regina   ● Winnipeg

● Thunder Bay

Quebec ○

St. Lawrence

○ Halifax

ATES   OF   AMERICA

L. Superior

L. Huron

Montreal ○

OTTAWA ○

Toronto

Hamilton ○

Lake Ontario

Niagara Falls

Windsor ○

Lake Erie

Wheat country
Great wheat hoppers where grain is stored are a familiar sight along the railroad in the Canadian prairies. Saskatchewan alone grows almost a tenth of the world's entire wheat crop.

Miles 0   150   300   450   600

Kilometres 0   150   300   450   600   750   900

Toronto
Toronto is Canada's largest metropolitan area with over 4 m people. When it was founded in 1793, it was called York, but it was renamed Toronto in 1834 after the Huron Indian word for a meeting place. Its most prominent landmark is the Canada National Tower, built in 1976. At 553 m, it is the world's tallest self-supporting structure.

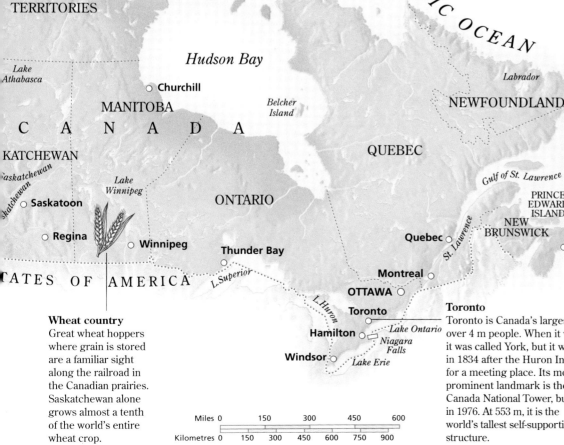

M   N   O   P   Q   R   S   T   U   V   W

Did you know? The Vikings briefly established a colony in Newfoundland 1000 years ago.

19

Did you know? Dutch settlers bought Manhattan Island from the Algonquin Native Americans in 1626 for just $24 worth of goods.

FACE THE FACTS...

❖ **Land**

Highest peak: Mt Mitchell, North Carolina (2037 m). Longest river: the Mississippi (3778 km).

❖ **State populations**

Alabama 4.4 m;
Delaware 783,000;
District of Columbia 572,000; Florida 15.9 million; Georgia 8.1 million; Illinois 12.4 m; Indiana 6 m;Kentucky 4 m; Maine 1.2 m; Maryland 5.2 m; Massachusetts 6.3 m; Michigan 9.9 m; Mississippi 2.8 m; New Hampshire 1.2 m; New Jersey 8.4 m; New York 18.9 m; North Carolina 8 million; Ohio 11.3 m; Pennsylvania 12.2 m; Rhode Island 1 m; South Carolina 4 m; Tennessee 5.6 m; Vermont 608,000; Virginia 7 m; West Virginia 1.8 m; Wisconsin 5.3 m.

❖ **State capitals**

See the map.

❖ **Natural resources**

The Appalachian and Allegheny Mountains of Pennsylvania, West Virginia, and east Kentucky have huge amounts of coal and iron.The hills of the northeast provide granite, slate and asbestos. Michigan is rich in copper, iron, iodine and gypsum. Georgia has bauxite (aluminium ore), marble and turpentine.

❖ **Agriculture**

The northeast states grow fruit and vegetables. In New England they also raise dairy cows and poultry. In Kentucky, they raise cows. Tobacco is an important crop in Kentucky and the Carolinas. Alabama and Georgia produce huge quantities of peanuts. On the Mississippi plains is the cotton belt. Florida produces citrus fruits.

❖ **Forestry & fishing**

The forests of the Appalachians and the northeast supply paper industries in Georgia, Alabama and Maine. The Atlantic Ocean off New England teems with fish.

❖ **Industry**

The northeast is the most heavily industrialized region of the USA- the big cities have a huge range of industries. The motor industry thrives in Detroit; Massachusetts and New Jersey produce high-tech and electronic goods.

❖ **Government**

Each state has its own democratically elected federal government, and governor.

❖ **Religion**

Most are Protestant Christians.

❖ **Sport**

Baseball, American football.

USA – the eastern states

The eastern USA was the first part of North America settled by Europeans, and includes the 13 original states that formed the Union in 1776. The north is the most densely populated and heavily industrialized region of the USA, with big cities such as New York and Boston on the coast and Chicago and Detroit on the Great Lakes. The warmer south contains the cotton belt. Running down the middle are the wooded ridges of the Appalachian Mountains, separating the coastal plain from the plains of Middle America.

Golden season

Autumn in the USA is called Fall, and in Maine it is one of the most spectacular times of year. Come October each year, the mists begin to drift over the landscape and the leaves on the trees turn a rich variety of reds, oranges, browns and golds.

New English life

New England is the far northeast of the USA, including the states of Massachusetts, New Hampshire, Connecticut, Maine and Vermont. Here are some of the oldest buildings in the USA, and there are many attractive small towns with pretty 18th and 19th century houses made from clapboard.

Manhattan

The skyscraper was born in New York with the Flat Iron Building in 1902. Manhattan's skyline is now famous for its high buildings, including the Empire State Building (381 m).

Niagara Falls

The Niagara Falls are two great falls, the American Falls and the Horseshoe Falls, formed where the Niagara River drops from Lake Erie to Lake Ontario. In the past they have attracted some spectacular stunts, including Blondin's tightrope walk across the falls in 1859, and Annie Taylor's trip over the falls in a barrel in 1901.

Motown

Detroit on the Great Lakes has long been the centre of the US automobile industry, the headquarters of Ford, Chrysler and General Motors. Founded in 1701 by Antoine de la Motha Cadillac, it is sometimes known as Motown, which is short for motor town. In the 1960s, it was famous for its black soul 'Motown' music.

Statue of Liberty, New York.

MAINE
Bangor
Augusta
Portland
VERMONT
NEW HAMPSHIRE
Concord
Montpelier
Burlington
MASSACHUSETTS
Boston
Worcester
Springfield
RHODE ISLAND
Providence
CONNECTICUT
Hartford
Albany
Syracuse
Rochester
Buffalo
NEW YORK
Hudson
NEW JERSEY
New York
Jersey City
Trenton
Philadelphia
DELAWARE
PENNSYLVANIA
Harrisburg
Pittsburgh
Lake Ontario
Niagara Falls
Lake Erie
Erie
Cleveland
Akron
Toledo
Detroit
Lansing
MICHIGAN
Grand Rapids
Lake Huron
Lake Michigan
CANADA
Lake Superior
Marquette
Green Bay
Milwaukee
WISCONSIN
Madison
Wisconsin
Rockford
Chicago
Gary
Fort
Illinois

GREENLAND
Baffin Bay
Hudson Bay
CANADA
ATLANTIC OCEAN
UNITED STATES OF AMERICA
MEXICO
Gulf of Mexico
GUATEMALA
COSTA RICA
PANAMA
COLOMBIA
VENEZUELA
Caribbean Sea
Mississippi
PACIFIC OCEAN
HAWAII

Old iron
Pittsburgh and the surrounding regions used to be the industrial powerhouse of America. The rich coal beds fed giant steelworks, which, in turn, supplied hundreds of heavy engineering plants. But falling demand for coal and alternative sources of steel have left many industrial centres here in decline, with vast areas of derelict land.

'Gator country
In the southern tip of Florida is a vast area of steamy, tropical mangrove and cypress forest and swamp called the Everglades. It was made a national park in 1947 and is home to many endangered species such as the alligator, the white egret and the bald eagle, the USA's national symbol.

Disney World
Disney World near Orlando in Florida is one of the world's largest and most spectacular theme parks.

Pizza
A huge number of Italians have emigrated to America in the last 150 years, and virtually every major city in the USA has its Italian area, where there are Italian shops and cafés selling Italian food. Many Italian dishes have become part of the American way of eating – none more so than the pizza, a thick, soft version of which was created in Chicago.

Elvis statue, Tennessee

is space for a square. In a full game, two teams of nine take it in turns to bat or field. The batter has three tries to hit the ball thrown by the pitcher – and must then try to run round all the bases before the ball is fielded. Once three players are out – by being 'struck out', failing to hit the ball, being run out or having their shot caught in the air – the side's innings is over.

Baseball
Baseball is one of the most popular sports in the USA, played by children wherever there

white. The White House is also the name used for the president's immediate staff.

The President's home
The White House in Washington DC is the official home of the president of the United States, built in 1792–9 in greyish-white limestone. It is called the White House because after it was burned by British troops in 1814, the smoke-stained walls were painted

become 'no-go' areas at night for many white people.

The eastern Americans

Lifestyles vary tremendously within the eastern USA, from the hustle and bustle of New York, where life goes on 24 hours a day, to the quiet of the bayou, the backwaters of the south, where little can be heard but the slap of water.

Its extraordinary mixture of cultures and nationalities earned the USA the name 'Melting Pot'. But the mix

can sometimes lead to racial tensions. In big cities such as New York, where there are poor people of many races, resentment often simmers between the generally wealthier whites and the black descendants of Africans brought to America as slaves, and also the poor Hispanics (people from Latin America), and Puerto Ricans. Predominantly black areas of New York, for example the Bronx, have

Stars and stripes
The USA is a federation of 50 separate states, each represented by a star on the country's flag, the 'stars and stripes'. Originally there were just 13, but as the European settlers spread westwards in the 19th century, new states were added. All but two are grouped together between the Atlantic and Pacific. The remaining two are Alaska, brought from Russia for 2 cents an acre, and the Pacific island chain of Hawaii.

Bronx

Miles 0   125   250
Kilometres 0 100 200 300 400

VIRGINIA
Richmond
Norfolk
Virginia Beach
Charleston
WEST VIRGINIA
Greensboro
Raleigh
NORTH CAROLINA
Mount Mitchell 2037m
Charlotte
Wilmington
Cape Fear
SOUTH CAROLINA
Columbia
Augusta
Charleston
Savannah
GEORGIA
Albany
Macon
Atlanta
Columbus
Montgomery
ALABAMA
Birmingham
Tallahassee
Mobile
Biloxi
Jackson
Meridian
MISSISSIPPI
Greenville
Memphis
TENNESSEE
Chattanooga
Nashville
Knoxville
Tennessee
KENTUCKY
Frankfort
Lexington
Louisville
Owensboro
Evansville
INDIANA
Cincinnati
Ohio
Springfield
ILLINOIS
Wabash
Alabama
Mississippi
APPALACHIAN MOUNTAIN
ATLANTIC OCEAN
GULF OF MEXICO
Jacksonville
FLORIDA
Lake Okeechobee
Tampa
St. Petersburg
Orlando
Cape Canaveral
Fort Lauderdale
Miami
Key West
Florida Keys
Straits of Florida

Did you know? Chicago has the busiest airport in world, the world's largest grain market and the biggest US Mail Office.

Did you know? Some people reckon that Americans eat more than 45,000 burgers a minute.

USA – the central states

Blazing hot in summer, icy cold in winter and often buffeted by tornadoes and blizzards, this zone of the USA has extreme weather, but the landscape – containing the Great Plains and their grain-growing prairies – is wide open and mostly flat, growing more wheat and maize than anywhere else on Earth.

Face the Facts

❖ The land
The tallest peak is Mt Elbert in Colorado (4399 m). The longest river is the Missouri (4317 km).

❖ State populations
Arkansas 2.6 m; Colorado 4.3 m; Iowa 2.9 m; Kansas 2.6 m; Louisiana 4.4 m; Minnesota 4.9 m; Missouri 5.5 m; Nebraska 1.7 m; New Mexico 1.8 m; North Dakota 642,000; Oklahoma 3.4 m; South Dakota 754,000; Texas 20.8 m.

❖ State capitals
See the map.

❖ Natural resources
The southern central states such as Texas, Oklahoma and New Mexico produce a great deal of oil and gas – Texas produces more than any other state except Alaska. Texas also has minerals such as sulphur, helium, graphite and bromine. New Mexico is rich in silver, gold, uranium, potassium salts, copper, zinc, molybdenum and lead as well as oil and gas. South Dakota is rich in gold, silver, beryllium and bentonite. North Dakota is a major source of coal. Minnesota has the world's largest opencast iron ore mine.

❖ Farming
This is North America's agricultural heartland. On the vast rolling plains, huge amounts of wheat and maize are grown in the damper east and millions of beef cattle are raised on the ranches of the drier west. In warm Texas, there are plantations of rice, sugar cane and cotton in the east, and citrus fruit in the valley of the Rio Grande. Lousiana is known as the Sugar State. Further north, in the Dakotas and Iowa, the livestock and cereals are supplemented by sunflowers and beans.

❖ Industry
Most of central USA is agricultural, with industry confined to the major cities. But the combination of oil wealth and aerospace has drawn high-tech industries to Texan cities such as Houston, Dallas and San Antonio. Minneapolis-St Paul in Minnesota is a major processing centre for surrounding farmland, and home to the electronics giant, 3M.

❖ Government
Each of the states has its own democratically elected federal government, and governor.

❖ Religion
The majority of people in central USA are Protestant Christians, but there are many different sects. The largest single religion is Roman Catholicism.

❖ Sport
The big sports are baseball, American football, basketball and squash.

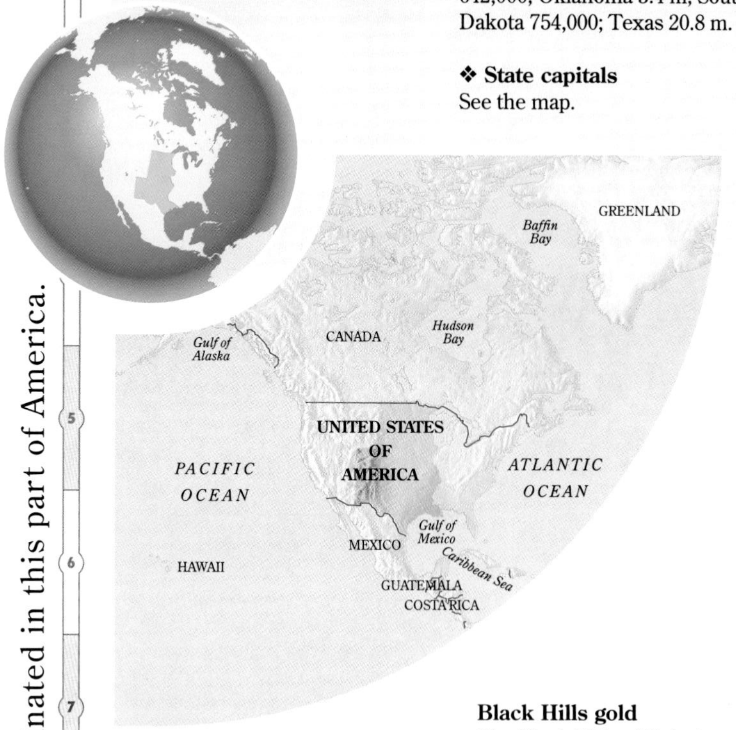
GREENLAND
Baffin Bay
Hudson Bay
CANADA
Gulf of Alaska
UNITED STATES OF AMERICA
PACIFIC OCEAN
ATLANTIC OCEAN
Gulf of Mexico
MEXICO
Caribbean Sea
HAWAII
GUATEMALA
COSTA RICA

Cliff faces
High in the granite face of Mount Rushmore in Dakota's Black Hills are carved colossal heads of US presidents Washington, Jefferson, Lincoln and Theodore Roosevelt. They were hewn from the rock between 1927 and 1939 by sculptor Gutzon Borglum and are now a national monument.

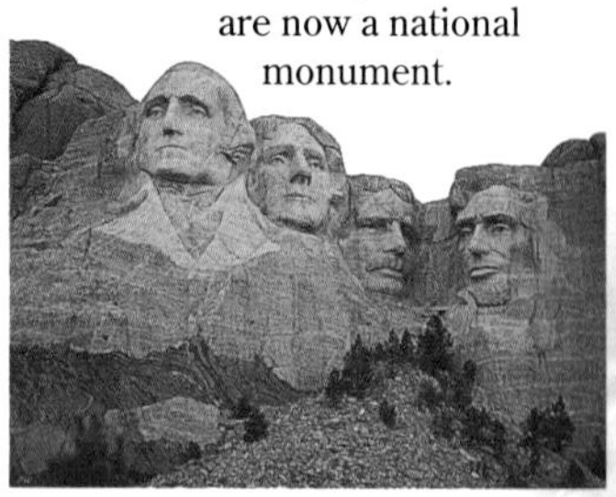

Black Hills gold
The Black Hills of Dakota became famous when gold was discovered here in 1874, sparking a gold rush.

Badlands
Deep gullies and ravines criss-cross the Badlands of Dakota and Nebraska, which got their name because French trappers in the 19th century found them bad lands to cross because of all their ups and downs.

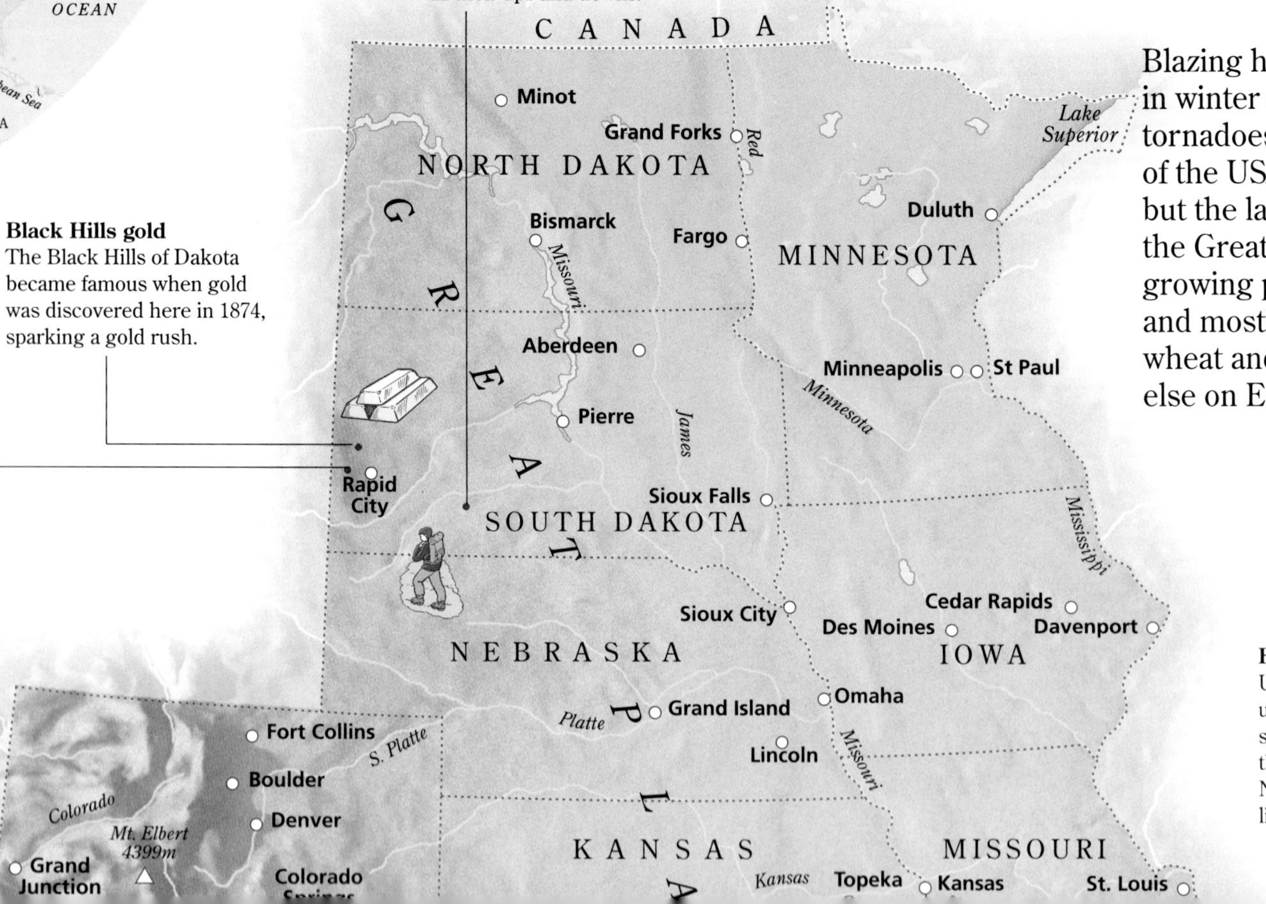
CANADA
Minot
Grand Forks
Red
NORTH DAKOTA
Bismarck
Fargo
Missouri
Lake Superior
Duluth
MINNESOTA
GREAT PLA
Aberdeen
Pierre
James
Minneapolis
St Paul
Minnesota
Rapid City
Sioux Falls
SOUTH DAKOTA
Mississippi
Sioux City
Des Moines
Cedar Rapids
Davenport
IOWA
NEBRASKA
Omaha
Platte
Grand Island
Lincoln
Fort Collins
S. Platte
Boulder
Denver
Colorado
Mt. Elbert 4399m
Grand Junction
Colorado Springs
KANSAS
Kansas
Topeka
Kansas
MISSOURI
St. Louis

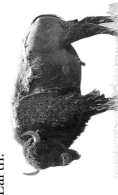

Buffalo
Until the 19th century, millions of buffalo used to roam the Great Plains. Herds several km long would thunder across the grass looking for fresh pasture. Now there are just 50,000 of them living on reserves.

Did you know? Mark Twain, the writer, was once a steamboat pilot on the Mississippi.

Did you know? Popcorn originated in this part of America.

Tornado Alley
Tornado Alley is a band running through Kansas, Oklahoma and Missouri, which is blasted by hundreds of tornadoes every year. Tornadoes are ferocious spirals of wind hanging down from a thundercloud. They are so powerful that they have been known to lift an entire train or shoot a wooden plank through steel.

Oil well
When oil was discovered in Texas in 1901, the state's fortune was made. Hundreds of oil wells were drilled. Two of the world's largest oil companies, Exxon and Amoco, were founded on Texan oil.

Spanish town
The Hispanic influence is potent in many parts of Texas, and more than half the population of San Antonio is Hispanic. The Spanish influence on the historic Paseo del Rio (river walk) is unmistakable.

Fast food
America is the home of fast food, and across the country there are millions of fast-food 'joints' selling old favourites such as milkshakes, hamburgers and Coca Cola.

richest cities on Earth, with more than its fair share of wealthy people. Oil, high-tech weapons and finance keep the money rolling in. For many people, Dallas is a place to shop, with its gigantic malls, the famous Neiman-Marcus store and Farmers' Market, the largest outdoor market in America.

Dallas style
In the 1970s, millions of people across Europe and America tuned in to watch the TV soap opera Dallas, based on a family of oil millionaires on their ranch near the city. Although the oil business is no longer the guarantee of wealth it used to

be, many people still have extremely lavish lifestyles.

Shopping city
Everything in Texas seems to be done on a grand scale and Dallas is no exception. It has the largest commercial airport in the world. It is also one of the

Americans of the central states

Far from the sea and from the world outside America, the 'middle' and southern Americans in small towns and on farms have a reputation for being conservative and inward looking. The legacy of hardship from the time of the Dust Bowl left a distrust of strangers in some places. However, cities such as Houston and San Antonio are among the most dynamic and sophisticated in the USA.

Cowboys
The ranches of the Great Plains are one of the few places were cowboys survive, looking after vast herds of cattle. But many fly in a helicopter or steer a jeep rather than ride a horse.

Dust bowl
Removing the protective covering of grass can leave the soil very vulnerable to the winds that whip across this open landscape. In the 1930s, heavy farming so exposed the soil of the prairies that the entire topsoil was stripped away, leaving just dust over a vast area called the Dust Bowl. The Dust Bowl once covered an area the size of Ireland, and drove many farmers to ruin. Irrigation, regrassing and windbreaks are now essential.

Combine harvester
Bringing in the harvest is a massive task on the Great Plains, but it can be done with the help of machinery. The huge, flat fields make mechanized harvesting on a giant scale relatively easy, and teams of massive combined harvesters bring in the grain as quickly as possible.

Beneath the prairie
Much of the prairies was once undermined by the fantastic communal burrows of the ground squirrel called the prairie dog. One was 150 km wide and 400 km long and contained 400 million prairie dogs. Farmers have now eradicated huge numbers of these small animals.

Springfield

Memphis

ARKANSAS

Little Rock

Greenville

Shreveport

Arkansas

Red

LOUISIANA

Baton Rouge

New Orleans

Port Arthur

Mississippi Delta

Mississippi

GULF OF MEXICO

Galveston

Beaumont

Houston

Corpus Christi

Laredo

San Antonio

Austin

Waco

Dallas

Fort Worth

Abilene

San Angelo

TEXAS

Rio Grande

Colorado

Brazos

Pecos

Big Spring

Midland

Odessa

Lubbock

Amarillo

Las Cruces

El Paso

Roswell

Santa Fe

Albuquerque

NEW MEXICO

Rio Grande

MEXICO

Canadian

Red

Lawton

Oklahoma City

OKLAHOMA

Tulsa

Fort Smith

Wichita Falls

Cimarron

Wichita

N
S

OZARK PLAT

Fort Smith

| Miles | 0 | | 125 | | 250 |
| Kilometres | 0 | 100 | 200 | 300 | 400 |

Did you know? Arkansas was the last state to keep black children and white children separate in schools.

Did you know? Death Valley, a desert area in California, is appropriately named: it is one of the hottest, driest places in the world.

FACE THE FACTS

❖ Land
The highest peak on this map is Mt Whitney in the Sierra Nevada in California (4418 m). Denali (Mt McKinley) in Alaska is higher still (6194 m). The Colorado (2253 km) is the longest river.

❖ State populations
Arizona 5.1 m; California 33.8 m; Idaho 1.2 m; Montana 902,000; Nevada 2 m; Oregon 3.4 m; Utah 2.2 m; Washington 5.8 m; Wyoming 493,000.

❖ State capitals
See the map.

❖ Natural resources
In the Rocky Mountains there is a wealth of mineral resources that make the USA a major producer of copper, lead, iron ore, gold, silver, molybdenum, uranium and vanadium. There are also substantial oil and natural gas reserves in California. Wyoming is the USA's main coal source.

❖ Forestry
Almost a third of the USA is still covered with forest, and much of it is in the west, where despite heavy logging there are still vast forests of cedar and fir.

❖ Agriculture
The warmth and fertility of California's soil enable it to grow huge amounts of cotton and grapes, if properly irrigated. This state produces by itself half of the USA's fruit and vegetables, including peaches, oranges, plums, avocados and almonds. Washington and Oregon are major fruit growers, too. Beef cattle are raised on the foothills of Utah.

❖ Industry
High-tech industries such as computers and aircraft are big in the western USA. Silicon Valley near San Francisco is one of the world's major electronics centres. California is also a major maker of military aircraft, while Seattle in Washington is the home of Boeing, the world's largest aircraft makers, as well as Microsoft, the world's biggest computer software company.

❖ Government
Each of the states has its own democratically elected federal government, and governor.

❖ Religion
The majority of people in the Western USA are Protestant Christians, but there are many different sects, including the Mormons based at Salt Lake City in Utah. But the largest single religion is Roman Catholicism.

❖ Sport
The big sports are baseball, American football, basketball and squash.

USA – the western states

The western side of the USA is very mountainous. Nowhere but in the coastal valleys of the Pacific states does it drop much below 1000 m, and the highest peaks of the Rockies, the Cascades and the Sierra Nevada soar to over 4000 m. Much of the land is wilderness, yet huge numbers of people live in the coastal states.

Going Boeing
Named after a Native American chief, Seattle was first set up as a logging camp 150 years ago. Now it is a major industrial centre with shipyards and high-tech industry including computer software giants Microsoft and Boeing, the world's biggest aircraft makers.

Timber wolf
The forests of the Rocky Mountains are one of the few remaining strongholds of the timber wolf. Looking a little like Alsatian dogs, they live in social groups and hunt in packs for animals such as elks.

Golden Gate Bridge
The Golden Gate in San Francisco, one of the world's most famous bridges, is named after the gold rush of 1849 in which thousands of prospectors came here hoping to make their fortunes. San Francisco is now one of the most attractive cities in the USA, and overlooks a beautiful natural harbour.

Yellowstone
Yellowstone National Park, on the borders of Wyoming, Idaho and Montana, is one of the world's oldest national parks, designated in 1872. It was the scene of what may have been one of the biggest volcanic eruptions ever, some two million years ago. The photo shows a geyser – a naturally

Map labels:
ARCTIC OCEAN
GREENLAND
Baffin Bay
Hudson Bay
ATLANTIC OCEAN
CANADA
UNITED STATES OF AMERICA
Gulf of Mexico
MEXICO
Beaufort Sea
ALASKA
Gulf of Alaska
Bering Sea
PACIFIC OCEAN
HAWAII

CANADA
WASHINGTON
Cape Flattery
Seattle
Tacoma
Olympia
Columbia
Mt. Rainier 4392m
Mount St. Helens 2550m
Portland
Salem
Eugene
Yakima
Richland
Pendleton
Bend
Spokane
Snake
OREGON
CASCADE RANGES
Medford
Klamath
PACIFIC OCEAN
Eureka
IDAHO
Boise
Lewiston
Twin Falls
Idaho Falls
Pocatello
Snake
MONTANA
Missoula
Butte
Helena
Great Falls
Billings
Miles City
Missouri
ROCKY MOUNTAINS
WYOMING
YELLOWSTONE NATIONAL PARK
Yellowstone
Sheridan
Powder
Casper

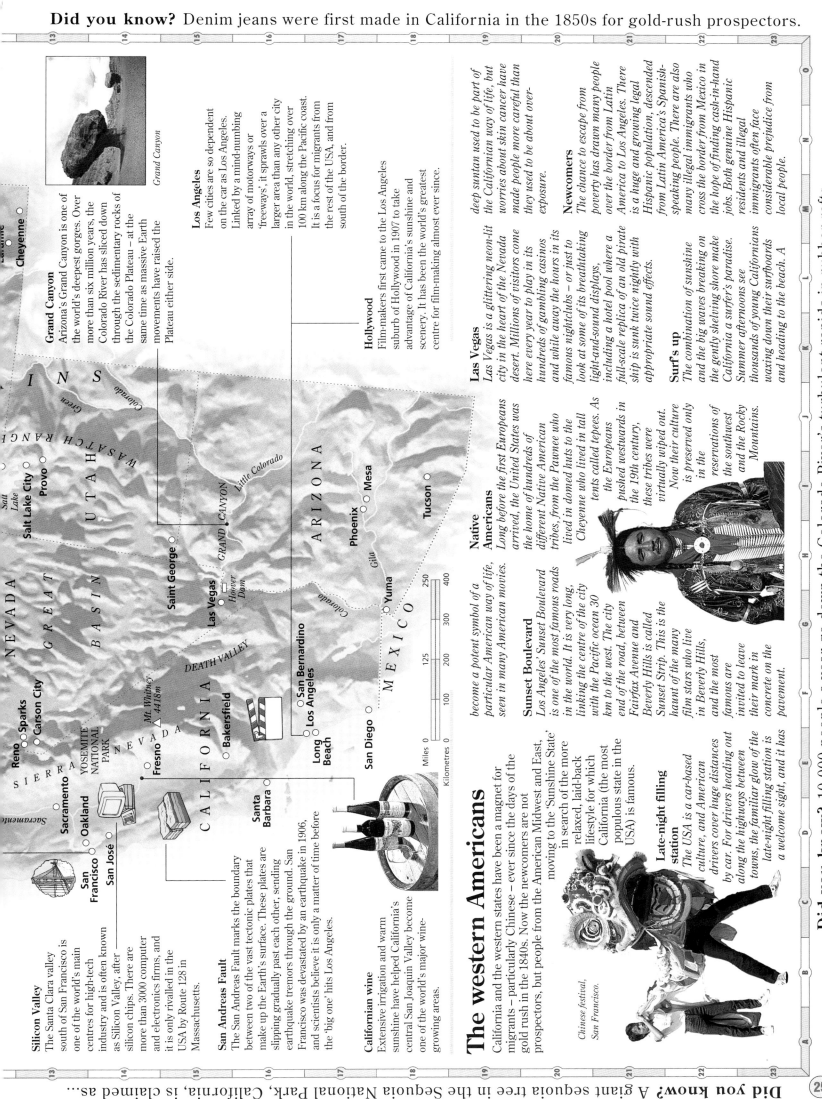

Grand Canyon

Silicon Valley
The Santa Clara valley south of San Francisco is one of the world's main centres for high-tech industry and is often known as Silicon Valley, after silicon chips. There are more than 3000 computer and electronics firms, and it is only rivalled in the USA by Route 128 in Massachusetts.

San Andreas Fault
The San Andreas Fault marks the boundary between two of the vast tectonic plates that make up the Earth's surface. These plates are slipping gradually past each other, sending earthquake tremors through the ground. San Francisco was devastated by an earthquake in 1906, and scientists believe it is only a matter of time before the 'big one' hits Los Angeles.

Californian wine
Extensive irrigation and warm sunshine have helped California's central San Joaquin Valley become one of the world's major wine-growing areas.

Grand Canyon
Arizona's Grand Canyon is one of the world's deepest gorges. Over more than six million years, the Colorado River has sliced down through the sedimentary rocks of the Colorado Plateau – at the same time as massive Earth movements have raised the Plateau either side.

Los Angeles
Few cities are so dependent on the car as Los Angeles. Linked by a mind-numbing array of motorways or 'freeways', it sprawls over a larger area than any other city in the world, stretching over 100 km along the Pacific coast. It is a focus for migrants from the rest of the USA, and from south of the border.

Hollywood
Film-makers first came to the Los Angeles suburb of Hollywood in 1907 to take advantage of California's sunshine and scenery. It has been the world's greatest centre for film-making almost ever since.

Las Vegas
Las Vegas is a glittering neon-lit city in the heart of the Nevada desert. Millions of visitors come here every year to play in its hundreds of gambling casinos – or just to look at some of its breathtaking light-and-sound displays, including a hotel pool where a full-scale replica of an old pirate ship is sunk twice nightly with appropriate sound effects.

Surf's up
The combination of sunshine and the big waves breaking on the gently shelving shore make California a surfer's paradise. Summer afternoons see thousands of young Californians waxing down their surfboards and heading to the beach. A

deep suntan used to be part of the Californian way of life, but worries about skin cancer have made people more careful than they used to be about over-exposure.

Newcomers
The chance to escape from poverty has drawn many people over the border from Latin America to Los Angeles. There is a huge and growing legal Hispanic population, descended from Latin America's Spanish-speaking people. There are also many illegal immigrants who cross the border from Mexico in the hope of finding cash-in-hand jobs. Both genuine Hispanic residents and illegal immigrants often face considerable prejudice from local people.

Native Americans
Long before the first Europeans arrived, the United States was the home of hundreds of different Native American tribes, from the Pawnee who lived in domed huts to the Cheyenne who lived in tall tents called tepees. As the Europeans pushed westwards in the 19th century, these tribes were virtually wiped out. Now their culture is preserved only in the reservations of the southwest and the Rocky Mountains.

become a potent symbol of a particular American way of life, seen in many American movies.

Sunset Boulevard
Los Angeles' Sunset Boulevard is one of the most famous roads in the world. It is very long, linking the centre of the city with the Pacific ocean 30 km to the west. The city end of the road, between Fairfax Avenue and Beverly Hills, is called Sunset Strip. This is the haunt of the many film stars who live in Beverly Hills, and the most famous are invited to leave their mark in concrete on the pavement.

The western Americans
California and the western states have been a magnet for migrants – particularly Chinese – ever since the days of the gold rush in the 1840s. Now the newcomers are not prospectors, but people from the American Midwest and East, moving to the 'Sunshine State' in search of the more relaxed, laid-back lifestyle for which California (the most populous state in the USA) is famous.

Late-night filling station
The USA is a car-based culture, and American drivers cover huge distances by car. For drivers heading out along the highways between towns, the familiar glow of the late-night filling station is a welcome sight, and it has

Chinese festival, San Francisco.

Map labels
Cheyenne

NEVADA
GREAT BASIN
Reno
Sparks
Carson City
SIERRA NEVADA
Sacramento
Oakland
San Francisco
San José
YOSEMITE NATIONAL PARK
Fresno
Mt. Whitney 4418m
DEATH VALLEY
Bakersfield
Santa Barbara
San Bernardino
Los Angeles
Long Beach
San Diego
CALIFORNIA

UTAH
WASATCH RANGE
Salt Lake
Salt Lake City
Provo
Green
Colorado
Saint George
Little Colorado
Las Vegas
Hoover Dam
GRAND CANYON
Colorado
Gila
Phoenix
Mesa
Tucson
Yuma
ARIZONA

MEXICO

Miles 0 | 125 | 250
Kilometres 0 | 100 | 200 | 300 | 400

Did you know? 10,000 people a year go down the Colorado River's turbulent rapids in rubber rafts.

Central America & the Caribbean

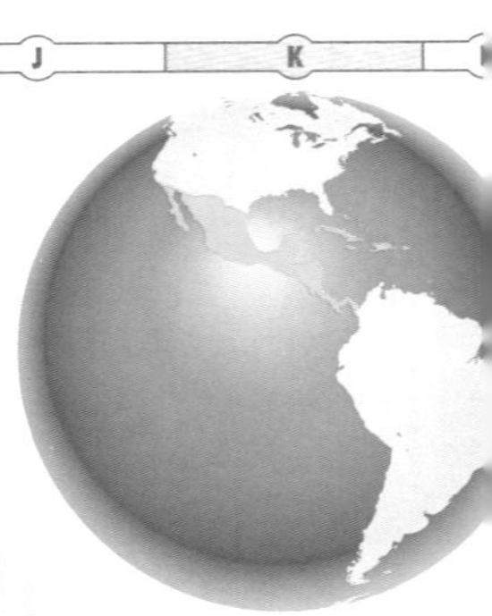

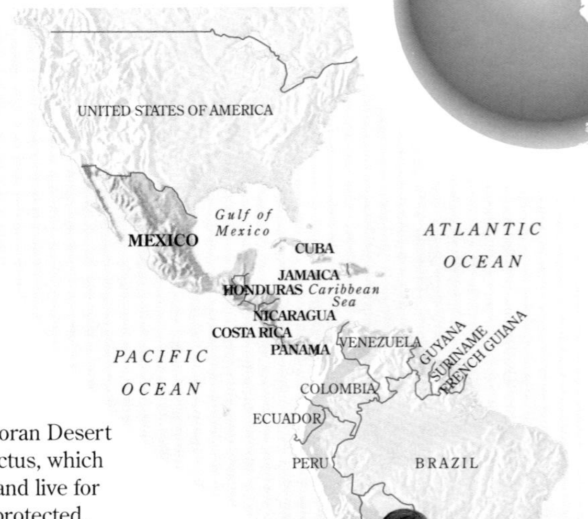

The islands of the Caribbean and the countries of Central America look like tropical paradises, but they have a chequered history. When the Europeans came here in 1492, they all but wiped out the Native Americans, then brought slaves from Africa, and finally left behind political turmoil. Most places are now relatively free from trouble, but too many people are very poor.

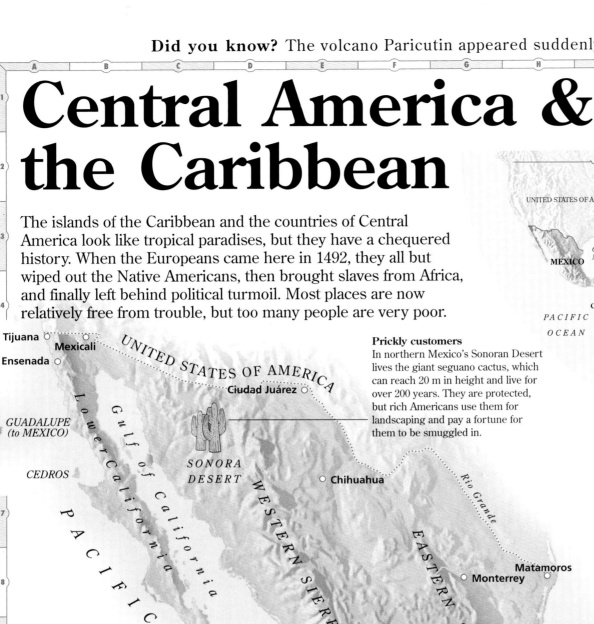

Prickly customers
In northern Mexico's Sonoran Desert lives the giant seguano cactus, which can reach 20 m in height and live for over 200 years. They are protected, but rich Americans use them for landscaping and pay a fortune for them to be smuggled in.

Mexico City
Sitting 2100 m above sea level, Mexico City is the sprawling, dirty, energetic heart of Mexico – and may be the fastest growing city in the world. There are already more than 20 million people here and each week 10,000 more people crowd in to find work – and scrabble for living space in the city's shanty towns or *cuidades perdidas* (lost cities).

The Central Americans

There is a wide mix of people in this region. On many islands in the Caribbean most people are the descendants either of African slaves or of Spanish settlers. In Central America most people are *mestizo* – the descendants of both Spanish settlers and Native Americans.

Mestizos and Native Americans
Most of Mexico's people are mestizos, *but there are still more than 15 m Native Americans. Officially, the government promotes Native American culture, but many Native Americans live in villages away from the mainstream of Mexican life, and their encounters with security forces are not always friendly.*

The Spanish flavour
The influence of Spain is everywhere. The main language in countries such as Mexico and Cuba is Spanish, and the Spanish style is unmistakable in buildings.

Reggae music
Music is important to the African peoples of the Caribbean, and many a warm tropical night echoes to the throbbing beat of reggae and the lively rhythm of calypso. Reggae is especially big in Jamaica, where black American dance music has also become a major influence. Jamaica was the home of the singer Bob Marley, who died of cancer in 1981 aged just 36.

Heavy traffic
Mexico City is chock-full of cars and traffic snarl-ups are part of the way of life. So, unfortunately, is pollution, for the mountains around the city trap exhaust fumes and smoke from factories, leaving it almost permanently shrouded in light smog. Authorities have tried to reduce pollution by banning cars with certain number plates from the city on certain days.

Cornucopia
Maize (corn) has been the staple food in Mexico for more than 7000 years. Today, Mexicans eat tortillas, pancakes made from cornflour, often bought from street vendors who cook them on a big, round flat hotplate. Tortillas are typically filled with meat or beans and salad as tacos, or rolled up as enchiladas.

Map labels: UNITED STATES OF AMERICA; Gulf of Mexico; MEXICO; CUBA; ATLANTIC OCEAN; JAMAICA; HONDURAS; Caribbean Sea; NICARAGUA; COSTA RICA; PANAMA; PACIFIC OCEAN; VENEZUELA; GUYANA; SURINAME; FRENCH GUIANA; COLOMBIA; ECUADOR; PERU; BRAZIL

Tijuana; Mexicali; Ensenada; UNITED STATES OF AMERICA; Ciudad Juárez; GUADALUPE (to MEXICO); CEDROS; Gulf of California; Lower California; SONORA DESERT; Chihuahua; WESTERN SIERRA MADRE; Rio Grande; EASTERN SIERRA MADRE; Matamoros; Monterrey; PACIFIC OCEAN; M E X I C O; San Luis Potosí; Tampico; GULF OF MEXICO; Aguascalientes; León; Guadalajara; Morelia; MEXICO CITY; Citlaltépetl 5700m; Gulf of Campeche; Mérida; Yucatán Peninsula; Toluca; Puebla; BELMOPAN; BELIZE; Balsas; Acapulco; Gulf of Tehuantapec; GUATEMALA; GUATEMALA; EL SALVADOR; SAN SALVADOR; Tropic of Cancer

FACE THE FACTS...

❖ The land
The highest peak in the region is the volcano Orizaba or Citlaltépetl in Mexico (5700 m); the longest river is Mexico's Rio Bravo (2100 km).

❖ Climate
The region lies entirely within the tropics, and near sea level, the climate is hot and steamy, with temperatures averaging well over 25°C (the *tierra caliente*). Higher up, though, the climate is more temperate.

❖ Population
The population of Central America and the Caribbean is 169 m, of whom 96 m live in Mexico. Cuba (11.1 m) and Guatemala (11 m) are the only other countries with populations over 10 m.

❖ Capitals
See the map.

❖ Natural resources
Mexico is rich in oil, natural gas, coal and hydroelectric potential. It also has gold, copper, lead, zinc, mercury, iron, and a fifth of the world's silver and a quarter of its fluorspar, used in steel-making. Jamaica has bauxite for aluminium. Panama has untapped copper reserves, and Honduras has copper, iron and tin.

❖ Farming
Mexico is mountainous and dry and only 12 per cent of the land is used for farming, but in the region as a whole volcanic ash has made the soil fertile. Where there is rain, giant plantations flourish, growing tobacco, coffee, sugar cane, cocoa, cotton, rubber, bananas and other tropical fruit. Farms grow beans, rice, and wheat and raise pigs and cattle – but in Mexico, most land is devoted to maize.

❖ Forestry
About 20 per cent of Mexico is covered in forests.

❖ Industry and commerce
Manufacturing industry is comparatively undeveloped in the region, except in Mexico. Mexico has a large steel industry, and 56 per cent of its export earnings come from manufactured goods – including cars.

❖ Government
The countries of Central America and the Caribbean were once colonies of European powers. Most have suffered corrupt government, military dictatorship or violent revolution. All but Belize are now republics of one kind or another, with, in theory at least, freely elected governments. Belize has its own government but its head of state is the British Queen.

❖ Religion
The vast majority of people in Central America are Roman Catholics. Voodoo is practised in Haiti and Rastafarianism in Jamaica.

❖ Language
In cities, most speak either English or Spanish (or French), but in the villages of Central America many people speak one of the Native American languages.

❖ Sport
Football, baseball and basketball.

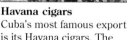

Havana cigars
Cuba's most famous export is its Havana cigars. The tobacco leaves are picked green, then hung for 45 days until yellow. They are then packed and allowed to ferment before being hand-rolled.

Castro's Cuba
Cuba was ruled by a dictator until the communist revolution led by Fidel Castro in 1959. Health care, housing and education all improved dramatically. Cuba used to rely heavily on the Soviet Union for aid and a special market for its sugar. When the Soviet Union broke up in 1991 this vital support was cut and Cuba's economy virtually collapsed. A rise in tourism is giving much-needed foreign earnings.

Wind tunnel
Most of the region lies right in the path of the half-a-dozen or so hurricanes that sweep across the Atlantic every year between May and October bringing devastation, torrential rain and floods.

Miles 0 — 100 — 200 — 300 — 400
Kilometres 0 — 100 — 200 — 300 — 400 — 500 — 600

BAHAMAS

ATLANTIC OCEAN

○ NASSAU

TURKS & CAICOS ISLANDS (to UK)

VIRGIN ISLANDS (to USA/UK)

ANTIGUA & BARBUDA

MONTSERRAT (to UK)

SAN JUAN

ST. KITTS & NEVIS

GUADELOUPE (to FRANCE)

HAVANA

CUBA Camagüey ○

DOMINICAN REPUBLIC

PUERTO RICO (to USA)

DOMÍNICA

HAITI

SANTO DOMINGO ○

MARTINIQUE (to FRANCE)

PORT-AU-PRINCE ○

GREATER ANTILLES

ST. LUCIA

CAYMAN ISLANDS (to UK)

BARBADOS

KINGSTON ○

JAMAICA

ST. VINCENT & THE GRENADINES

CARIBBEAN SEA

Sweet slavery
In the 1700s, Europe developed a sweet tooth, and hundreds of thousands of Africans were shipped to the Caribbean islands, also known as the West Indies, to work as slaves on the sugar plantations.

GRENADA

TRINIDAD & TOBAGO

Going bananas
Bananas are crucial to the economy of many of the countries in this part of the world. They form around 36 per cent of the entire exports of Honduras. They are grown mostly on the coastal lowlands, then cut while green and left to ripen while being shipped.

ARUBA (to NETHERLANDS)

LESSER ANTILLES

PORT OF SPAIN ○

NETHERLANDS ANTILLES (to NETHERLANDS)

HONDURAS

GUCIGALPA ○

NICARAGUA

MANAGUA ○

Lake Nicáragua

Coffee grounds
While bananas are the mainstay in the lowlands, coffee beans are the biggest earners in the highlands. When the cherries on the trees turn red, they are ripe for picking – the coffee bean is the stone inside the cherry. Coffee is vital to countries such as Nicaragua, Guatemala, Costa Rica, El Salvador and Jamaica.

SAN JOSÉ ○

COSTA RICA

Panama Canal ○ PANAMA

PANAMA

COLOMBIA

Short cut
The 80-km long Panama Canal cuts right through the narrowest part of Central America to link the Atlantic to the Pacific – and save ships an 18,000-km journey all the way round South America.

...of the dead visit their families – by making sweets in the shape of skulls and skeletons.

27

Northern South America

The heart of northern South America is the great river basin of the Amazon with its vast, humid rainforest, the richest natural habitat in the world. Around it to the west arch the great peaks of the Andes, their snows feeding the Amazon and its tributaries.

FACE THE FACTS…

❖ The land
The highest peaks in the region include Huascarán in Peru (6768 m) and Chimborazo in Ecuador (6276 m). The longest rivers are the Amazon (6439 km), and the Tocantins (2699 km).

❖ Climate
Tropical – the region straddles the equator. In Manaus, in the Amazon rainforest, temperatures average 27°C. Near the coast, and in the mountains, the weather

is cooler and more comfortable. In Quito, Ecuador, the temperature never rises above 22°C by day, nor falls below 8°C at night and there is 100 mm of rain every month.

❖ Population
Brazil 167.9 m; Colombia 41.5 m; Peru 25.2 m; Venezuela 23.7 m; Guyana 856,000; Suriname 413,000; French Guiana 157,000.

❖ Capitals
See the map.

❖ Natural resources
Northern South America (particularly Brazil) is rich in mineral deposits. Peru and Bolivia have lead, zinc, copper, iron and silver. Although production has fallen, Bolivia is still the world's fifth-largest tin producer. The discovery of oil under Venezuela's lake Maracaibo in the early 20th century turned it from one of America's poorest countries to one of its richest.

❖ Farming
Besides staple crops such as

maize, wheat and rice, the region grows huge quantities of tropical and Mediterranean crops. Brazil, for instance, is one of the world's leading growers of oranges, bananas, cocoa beans, soya and sugar cane. Brazil and Colombia are the world's leading coffee growers. Rubber is extracted from trees in the Brazilian rainforest.

❖ Forestry
Brazil is the second-largest timber producer in the world – not only of irreplaceable hardwoods from the Amazon rainforest

in the north – ebony, teak and mahogany – but also softwoods from the hills of the south, including Panama pine and eucalyptus.

❖ Industry and commerce
Brazil is South America's leading industrial nation. Industries clustered round São Paulo, Rio and Belo Horizonte include steel, oil, shipbuilding, carmaking, aircraft-construction, and food and drink processing. Other countries in this region rely mostly on farming and mining.

❖ Government
All these countries have had their share of military dictatorships, corrupt politicians and terrorist opposition. But each is now, in theory at least, a democratic republic with a president.

❖ Religion
The majority of people are Roman Catholic Christians.

❖ Sport
Football is the region's big sport.

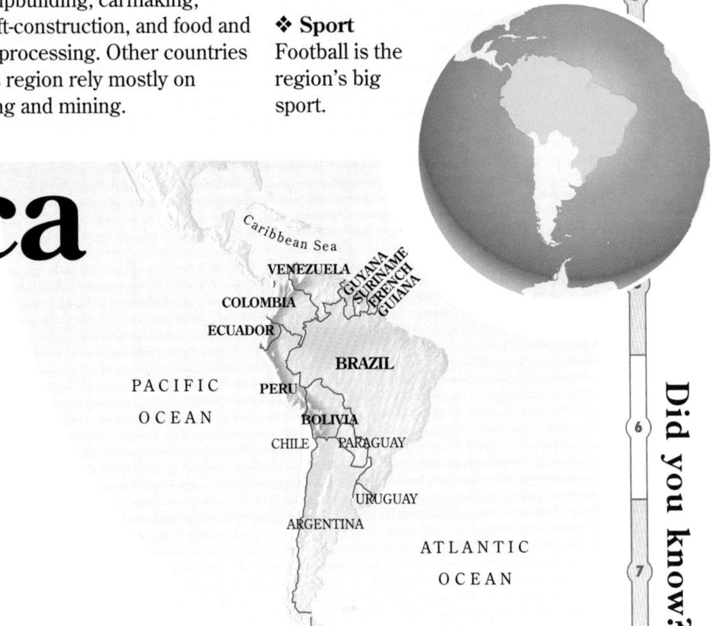

The Yanomani
The very existence of the Amazon's native peoples such as the Yanomani is threatened as their hunting grounds are taken over by white farmers and mining companies.

Green gem
The world's best emeralds come from the Chivor and Muzo mines in Colombia, first mined a thousand years ago by the Chibcha Indians. When the Spanish Conquistadors came to South America, they saw Incas in possession of Chivor emeralds, but they did not find the mines until 1537. Many of the famous emeralds brought to Spain early in the 16th century were stolen from the Incas.

Forest in danger
The Amazon rainforest is home to thousands of species of butterfly. But the forest is being cut for wood and burned to make way for roads, farms and mines at a frightening rate. An area the size of Ireland has been destroyed since 1990. The last forest-dwelling Indian tribes are threatened with extinction and the consequences of the loss of trees for the world's atmosphere are incalculable.

Toucan play
The toucan is just one of many curious species of bird that live in the canopy of the Amazon rainforest. Others include colourful macaws, glorious birds of paradise and hummingbirds. The best-known kind of toucan is the Toco Toucan, with its great yellow beak for grasping large fruit. The beak is very light - full of air holes to stop the bird overbalancing.

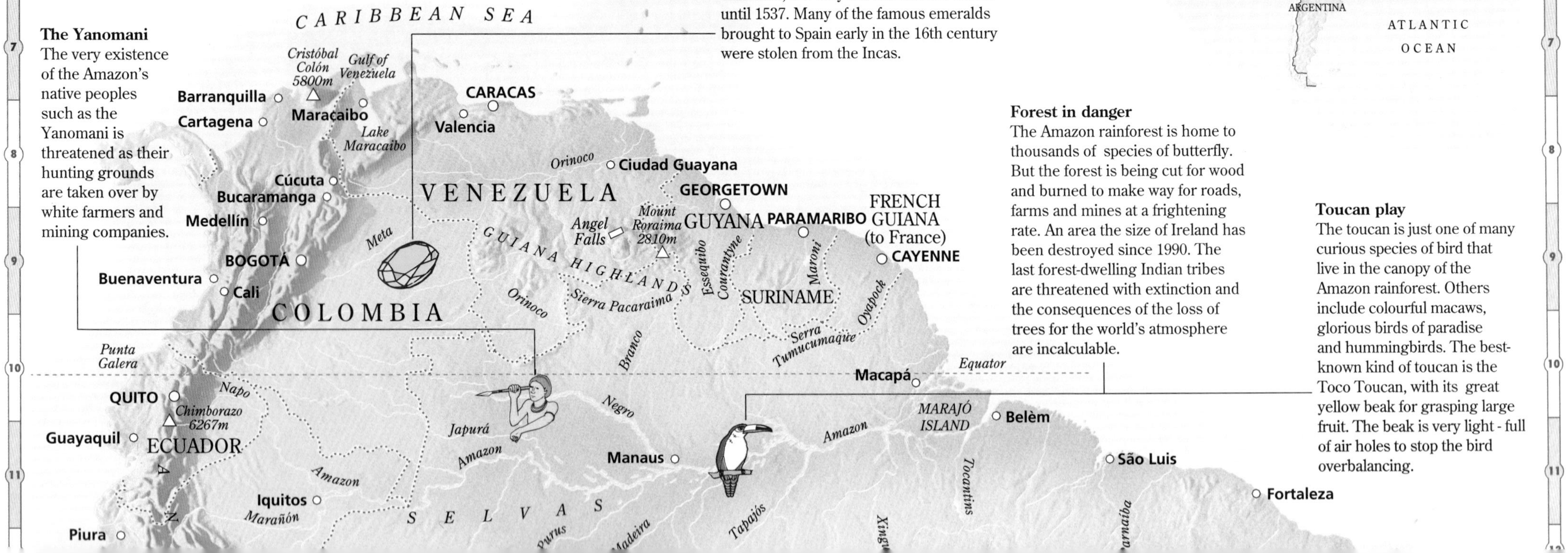

Map labels: ATLANTIC OCEAN, GUYANA, SURINAME, FRENCH GUIANA, VENEZUELA, COLOMBIA, ECUADOR, PERU, BRAZIL, BOLIVIA, PARAGUAY, CHILE, URUGUAY, ARGENTINA, Caribbean Sea, PACIFIC OCEAN

Map labels: CARIBBEAN SEA, Cristóbal Colón 5800m, Gulf of Venezuela, Lake Maracaibo, Maracaibo, Barranquilla, Cartagena, Cúcuta, Bucaramanga, BOGOTÁ, Medellin, Cali, Buenaventura, COLOMBIA, Meta, CARACAS, Valencia, VENEZUELA, Orinoco, Ciudad Guayana, GEORGETOWN, GUYANA, PARAMARIBO, SURINAME, FRENCH GUIANA (to France), CAYENNE, Mount Roraima 2810m, GUIANA HIGHLANDS, Sierra Pacaraima, Essequibo, Courantyne, Maroni, Oyapock, Serra Tumucumaque, Branco, Negro, Orinoco, Manaus, Equator, MARAJÓ ISLAND, Macapá, Belém, SELVAS, Amazon, Japurá, Iquitos, Marañón, Napo, Chimborazo 6267m, QUITO, ECUADOR, Guayaquil, Punta Galera, Piura, Tocantins, Xingu, São Luis, Fortaleza, Angel Falls

The northern South Americans

In this region, the rich few live side by side with the very, very poor. In cities such as Lima, Rio and Caracas, swish modern apartments overlook *calampas*, *barrios* and *favelas*, the shanty towns built from scrap. All these countries are starting to do better, but some governments owe so much money to banks in Europe, America and Japan that they often cannot afford to pay for new developments.

Peruvian Indians
Peru's three million Amerindians, mainly Quechua and Aymará, live in the countryside, almost completely separate from the mestizos (mixed European and Indian) and people of European descent who live in the towns and cities. When they come to town, the Indians often suffer discrimination.

Playing for kicks
In Brazil, street football or *pelado* is played by children everywhere – in the streets, in backyards, on the beach, sometimes with a ball, sometimes with a tin can, sometimes with a coconut. The rules are slightly different from normal football, but the passion for the game is unmistakable. There are more than 20,000 football teams in Brazil, and Rio's Maracaña Stadium is the biggest in the world.

Carnival
For four days and nights in Lent (February/March). Rio de Janeiro goes wild with its annual carnival. All over the city, people prepare months in advance, creating spectacular costumes and floats. Day and night, the streets are crammed with people dancing, singing and generally having a riotous time – and everywhere there is the rhythm of the samba, Rio's own special dance.

A good reed
The great lake of Titicaca in Bolivia, at an altitude of 3812 m, is the world's highest navigable lake. It is still plied by the reed boats of the Urus, who live on rafts made from the reeds which grow in the lake.

Llama and alpaca
Related to the camel, the llama and the alpaca can survive high in the Andes mountains of Peru. Here on the Altiplano (high plain), where it is too cold to grow crops, they have been reared by the Native Indians for centuries for their fur and hide; their droppings make fuel.

Sugar Loaf Mountain
The distinctive Sugar Loaf Mountain overlooks Rio de Janeiro, home to more than 12 m people and one of the world's ten biggest cities.

Preparing for take-off
Brazil's capital, Brasilia, was built in the 1950s in an unpopulated region quite a long way inland in order to attract people away from the crowded coast. It was laid out in the shape of an aeroplane. Homes and businesses are in the wings, while the most impressive hotels are in the nose and the President's Palace in the tail.

Right, selling souvenirs, Uros Islands, Lake Titicaca, on the border of Peru and Bolivia.

Below left, Rio carnival dress

Shanty living
As more and more land is taken over for large plantations and ranches geared to selling produce abroad, land prices are rising. So many poor farmers have been forced to migrate to the cities – one reason why cities in this region are growing faster than anywhere else. The newcomers have little money and there is neither work nor housing for them. They are therefore forced to build their own tiny single room out of scrap in any small space they can find in the shanty towns – known as calampas in Peru, barrios in Colombia and favelas in Brazil. These slums have no electricity, no running water and no rubbish collection. Because of insanitary conditions, diseases are rife.

Alpacas

Machu Picchu, an Inca town in the Peruvian Andes, rediscovered in 1911

Map labels

Recife
Maceió
Aracaju
Salvador

ATLANTIC OCEAN

São Francisco
C A A T ...

Barragem de Sobradinho
São Francisco

BRAZILIAN HIGHLANDS

Pico da Bandeira △ 2894m
Belo Horizonte
Serra da Mantiqueira
São Paulo
Santos
Rio de Janeiro

BRASÍLIA

Paraná

MATO GROSSO PLATEAU
Arinos
Goiania
C A M P O S

Araguaia

SERRA DO MAR
Pôrto Alegre
Lagôa dos Patos
Itaipu Reservoir
Paraná
Lagôa Mirim
Campo Grande
Uruguai
Paraguay

PARAGUAY
URUGUAY

B R A Z I L

Guaporé
Mamoré
Beni
Madre de Dios

BOLIVIA
Cochabamba
Santa Cruz
Oruro
Sucre
Potosí
Poopó
Tarija
Pilcomayo

Arequipa
LA PAZ
Lake Titicaca
Nevado Sajama 6520m
ALTIPLANO

CHILE

P E R U
Cuzco
Huancayo
LIMA △
Callao
Huascarán 6768m △
Ucayali

PACIFIC OCEAN

Did you know? São Paulo has the largest Japanese community in the world outside Japan.

29

Did you know? Brazil supplies 85 per cent of the world's orange juice.

Did you know? The first soccer World Cup was held in Uruguay in 1930 – and Uruguay won.

FACE THE FACTS...

❖ **The land**
The highest peaks in the region are Aconcagua in Argentina (6960 m) and Ojos del Salado in Chile (6908 m). The longest river is the Paraná (4875 km).

❖ **Climate**
Southern South America stretches over an enormous latitude and the climate varies from the steamy tropical heat of Paraguay through the Mediterranean warmth of central Chile to the subarctic chill of Tierra del Fuego and the high peaks.

❖ **Population**
Argentina 36.5 m; Chile 15 m; Paraguay 5.3 m; Uruguay 3.3 m.

❖ **Capitals**
See the map.

❖ **Natural resources**
Both Chile and Argentina have big oil and gas reserves. Argentina also has a large coal mine at Río Turibio, plus significant deposits of zinc, lead, tungsten, iron, sulphur, mica and salt. Chile is rich in minerals such as copper, iron, gold and nitrates and has the world's only major natural source of nitrate of soda (Chile saltpetre).

❖ **Farming**
Much of southern South America is livestock country. Cows and, further south and higher up, sheep provide the backbone of the economy of Argentina and Uruguay. In Chile, most of the farms are in the central valley, where they grow cereals, vegetables, fruit, tobacco and hemp as well as raising cattle and sheep. Grapes grow well around Santiago, as do tomatoes, sunflowers and oranges. Paraguay grows cotton, cassava, soya and sugar cane.

❖ **Fishing**
The rich waters of the Pacific bring Chile the world's fifth-largest fish catch. Much of the fish is processed and turned into fish meal for fertilizer. Argentine and Uruguayan fishermen catch hake, anchovies and the dorado.

❖ **Industry and commerce**
Food-processing dominates Argentine industry – meat-packing, flour-milling, sugar-refining. But there are growing steel, car-making, aircraft-making, chemicals, textiles and electrical goods industries here too. Chile has a huge steelworks at Huachipato near Concepción. The other major industrial centre is Santiago.

❖ **Government**
With the exception of Uruguay, all these countries were not so long ago under the rule of military dictators – General Pinochet in Chile, General Galtieri in Argentina and General Stroessner in Paraguay. Now all are democratic republics.

❖ **Religion**
Most people are Roman Catholic Christians.

❖ **Sport**
Football is the big sport in the region. In Argentina, polo and car-racing are popular.

Big hole
Chile is the world's largest copper producer. The opencast copper mine at Chuquicamata near Calama in the Atacama Desert is one of the biggest man-made holes in the world. It is over 4 km long and 670 m deep, and every week millions of tonnes of rock are blasted from the ground. The world's largest deep copper mine is at El Teniente, southeast of Santiago.

Volcanic land
Chile is one of the most volcanically active countries, with 75 active volcanoes. The bed of the Pacific is sliding slowly under South America, sending huge globs of magma burning up through the Andes to create volcanic peaks. Eight of the world's tallest active volcanoes are here, including Osorno, pictured below, and the world's tallest, Guallatir (6170 m). In Argentina, Aconcagua, the world's highest peak outside the Himalayas, is a dormant volcano.

Osorno volcano, Chile.

Big dam
Seventy-five per cent of South America's power is hydroelectric. The hydroelectric power plant at Itaipú on the Brazil-Paraguay border on the Paraná River is the world's largest power station, capable of producing 12.6 billion megawatts of power. Itaipú is also one of the world's biggest dams and, when it was constructed, the lake behind it drowned one of the world's great waterfalls, the Guairá Falls.

Big beef
Cows are important in both Argentina and Uruguay, and on the vast ranches of the pampas huge herds of steers are reared for their beef and their hide. There are 50 million cows in Argentina alone, feeding both on the rich pasture and alfalfa mixed with grains of sorghum.

Giant anteater
The pampas is home to the weird-looking giant anteater with its incredibly long snout. The size of a leopard, this creature walks on its knuckles, so its claws are left sharp for digging. When it finds a termite mound, it will rip it open with its claws and suck up the insects using its snout like a vacuum cleaner.

Grass country
The pampas are the vast grasslands that cover more than a quarter of Argentina – over 650,000 sq km. The pampas is the heart of Argentine agriculture. In the humid west, cereal crops such as wheat and maize grow. But in the drier east there are vast cattle and sheep ranches.

Map labels

BRAZIL
BOLIVIA
PARAGUAY
URUGUAY
ARGENTINA
CHILE
GRAN CHACO
ATACAMA DESERT
SIERRA DE CÓRDOBA

Tropic of Capricorn

Arica
Iquique
Antofagasta
Copiapó
Coquimbo
San Juan
Mendoza
Valparaíso
Viña del Mar
SANTIAGO
Rancagua
Talca
Salta
San Miguel de Tucumán
Córdoba
Santa Fé
Parana
Rosario
BUENOS AIRES
La Plata
Concepción
ASUNCIÓN
Coronel Oviedo
Formosa
Corrientes
Ciudad del Este
Encarnación
Saltos
MONTEVIDEO

Itaipú
Itaipú Reservoir
Iguaçu Falls

Aconcagua 6960m
Tupungato 6800m
Llullaillaco 6723m
Ojos del Salado 6908m

Lake Mar Chiquita
Salado
Paraguay
Pilcomayo
Bermejo
Paraná
Uruguay
Negro
Río de La Plata

Southern South America

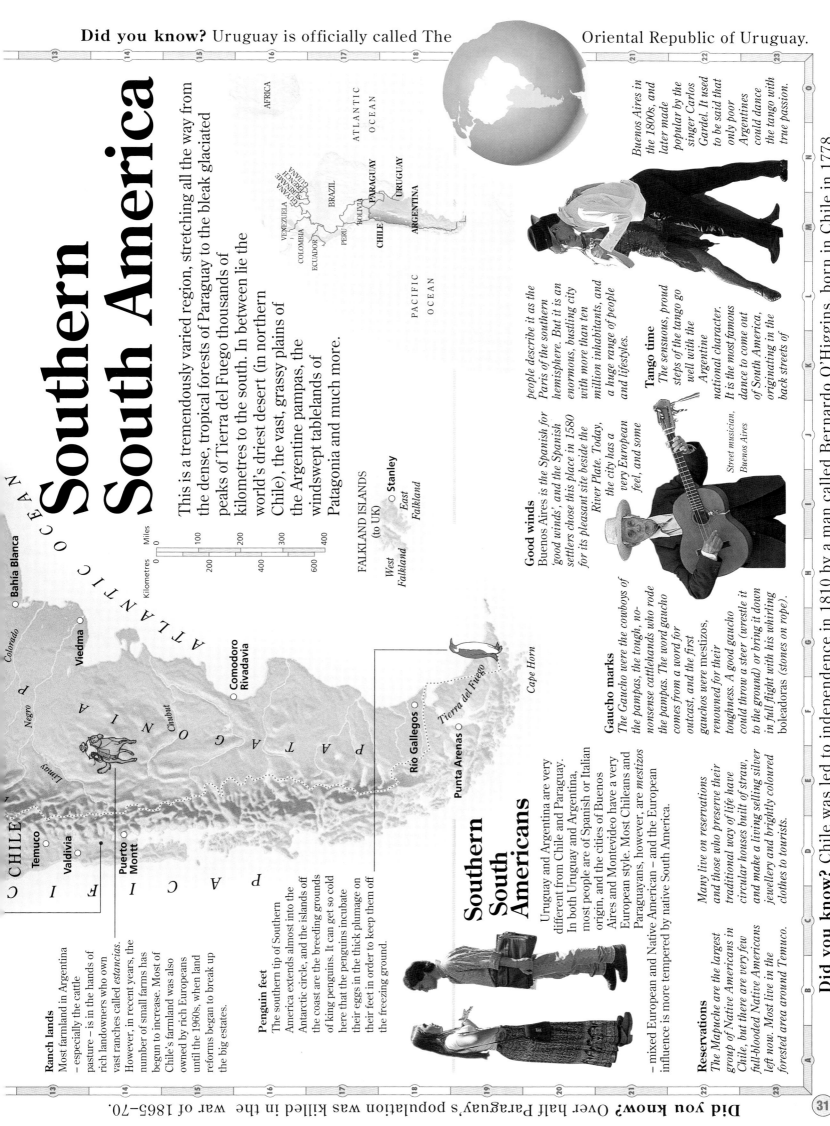

This is a tremendously varied region, stretching all the way from the dense, tropical forests of Paraguay to the bleak glaciated peaks of Tierra del Fuego thousands of kilometres to the south. In between lie the world's driest desert (in northern Chile), the vast, grassy plains of the Argentine pampas, the windswept tablelands of Patagonia and much more.

Ranch lands

Most farmland in Argentina – especially the cattle pasture – is in the hands of rich landowners who own vast ranches called *estancias*. However, in recent years, the number of small farms has begun to increase. Most of Chile's farmland was also owned by rich Europeans until the 1960s, when land reforms began to break up the big estates.

Penguin feet

The southern tip of Southern America extends almost into the Antarctic circle, and the islands off the coast are the breeding grounds of king penguins. It can get so cold here that the penguins incubate their eggs in the thick plumage on their feet in order to keep them off the freezing ground.

Southern South Americans

Uruguay and Argentina are very different from Chile and Paraguay. In both Uruguay and Argentina, most people are of Spanish or Italian origin, and the cities of Buenos Aires and Montevideo have a very European style. Most Chileans and Paraguayans, however, are mestizos – mixed European and Native American – and the European influence is more tempered by native South America.

Reservations

The Mapuche are the largest group of Native Americans in Chile, but there are very few full-blooded Native Americans left now. Most live in the forested area around Temuco.

Many live on reservations and those who preserve their traditional way of life have circular houses built of straw, and make a living selling silver jewellery and brightly coloured clothes to tourists.

Good winds

Buenos Aires is the Spanish for 'good winds', and the Spanish settlers chose this place in 1580 for its pleasant site beside the River Plate. Today, the city has a very European feel, and some people describe it as the Paris of the southern hemisphere. But it is an enormous, bustling city with more than ten million inhabitants, and a huge range of people and lifestyles.

Gaucho marks

The Gaucho were the cowboys of the pampas, the tough, no-nonsense cattlehands who rode the pampas. The word gaucho comes from a word for outcast, and the first gauchos were mestizos, renowned for their toughness. A good gaucho could throw a steer (wrestle it to the ground) or bring it down in full flight with his whirling boleadoras (stones on rope).

Street musician, Buenos Aires

Tango time

The sensuous, proud steps of the tango go well with the Argentine national character. It is the most famous dance to come out of South America, originating in the back streets of Buenos Aires in the 1800s, and later made popular by the singer Carlos Gardel. It used to be said that only poor Argentines could dance the tango with true passion.

Map labels

ATLANTIC OCEAN

PACIFIC OCEAN

CHILE

Bahia Blanca
Colorado
Negro
Viedma
Chubut
Comodoro Rivadavia
PATAGONIA
Rio Gallegos
Tierra del Fuego
Punta Arenas
Cape Horn

Temuco
Valdivia
Puerto Montt
Llanuy

FALKLAND ISLANDS (to UK)
West Falkland
East Falkland
Stanley

Miles
Kilometres
0 100 200 300 400
0 200 400 600

VENEZUELA
COLOMBIA
ECUADOR
PERU
BOLIVIA
BRAZIL
GUYANA
SURINAME
FRENCH GUIANA
PARAGUAY
URUGUAY
CHILE
ARGENTINA
AFRICA
ATLANTIC OCEAN
PACIFIC OCEAN

Did you know? Chile was led to independence in 1810 by a man called Bernardo O'Higgins, born in Chile in 1778.

Did you know? Over half Paraguay's population was killed in the war of 1865-70.

31

Europe

Europe, including European Russia, which extends as far as the Ural Mountains, is the second smallest continent. Only Australia is smaller. Europe has an irregular shape with long peninsulas, such as Iberia, Italy, Greece and Scandinavia, and many offshore islands. European Russia, together with Belarus and Ukraine, which are also parts of Europe, are shown on the map on pages 52–53.

Most western European countries already belong to the European Community, and more are gearing up to join. The European Community or EC was originally formed as a free trade zone, with no trade barriers. Now it is political as well. There is a European parliament in Brussels, and a single currency is being introduced. Whether this political and economic union can work is increasingly under debate; and whether a European super-state would help or hinder its member countries is one of the most important issues they have ever faced.

Roughly across the middle of Europe run a series of mountain chains including the Alps and the Pyrenees, which more or less divide the continent in two. To the south is Mediterranean Europe, with its warmish winters and hot, dry summers. To the north, is a much cooler, damper Europe extending far into the Arctic Circle where winter temperatures average well below freezing. But the coastal regions of northern Europe are unusually warm in winter for this latitude – similar to Labrador in Canada – because the chill is taken off by the warm waters of the Gulf Stream, the ocean current flowing across the Atlantic from the Caribbean.

European explorers boldly ventured out around the world in their small sailing boats in the 15th century, and for hundreds of years a few small western European countries – Portugal, Spain, France, Germany and Britain in particular – came to dominate the world to an astonishing degree. While Latin America became Spanish, the French and British established colonial rule over much of the rest of the world outside China and Russia. Britain controlled all the Indian subcontinent, much of Africa and all of Australia and New Zealand. Since World War II, the French and British have withdrawn from their colonies. Their dominance has been taken over by the USA, but they remain influential.

ARCTIC OCEAN

LAPLAND

Arctic Circle

NORWEGIAN SEA

KJØLEN MOUNTAINS

SWEDEN   FINLAND

Gulf of Bothnia

NORWAY

OSLO○

HELSINKI○

STOCKHOLM○   ○TALLINN

○Göteborg

BALTIC SEA

ESTONIA

LATVIA

○RIGA

ENMARK

OPENHAGEN○

LITHUANIA

RUSSIA VILNIUS○

Elbe

BERLIN○   WARSAW
○

ERMANY   POLAND

○PRAGUE

Danube   CZECH REP.   CARPATHIAN MOUNTAIN   Dniester

SLOVAKIA

TZER-   VIENNA ○   ○BRATISLAVA   MOLDOVA
D
S   AUSTRIA   ○BUDAPEST   Prut ○CHISINAU

HUNGARY

LJUBLJANA
○   ZAGREB
SLOVENIA ○CROATIA   ROMANIA

SAN MARINO   BOSNIA & ○BELGRADE   ○BUCHAREST   BLACK SEA
○   HERZEGOVINA
SARAJEVO○

ITALY   YUGOSLAVIA○SOFIA   BULGARIA

○ROME   ○SKOPJE

TIRANA○ MACEDONIA

ALBANIA

GREECE

R   SICILY   ATHENS○
A
N
E
A   MALTA
N

SEA   CRETE

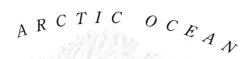

Europe includes some of the richest countries in the world. If the national income or GNP of Switzerland, for instance, is divided equally among all the country's people, they have more money than people in any other country in the world – including the United States. But there are also some very poor people in Europe – not only in the east, where communist rule left many people in desperate circumstances, but also in every western European country too. One fifth of the population of the UK, for instance, is estimated to be poor, even though most people are comfortably off.

Estonia, Latvia and Lithuania, although part of Europe, are such close neighbours of Russia that they are shown in detail on pages 52-53.

The Industrial Revolution began in western Europe, more than 200 years ago, and has spread around the world from here. Since World War II, traditional European industries such as coal-mining, steel-making, car-making and shipbuilding have suffered from competition from the rising economies of Asia. But Europe is still one of the world's most productive regions economically.

Europe has a long and varied history. There are dozens of countries packed into this small continent, each with its own unique culture and history, from tiny San Marino, one of the world's smallest countries, to Germany, recently a unified country for the first time in history. But one of the most remarkable things about the Europeans is the impact they have had on the world.

Britain & Ireland

The British Isles are made up of more than 4000 islands and have over 20,000 km of coastline. The Republic of Ireland is a separate state. Great Britain is the name used for the union of the three once-independent countries, England, Scotland and Wales. The United Kingdom is Great Britain plus the province of Northern Ireland. England is the biggest and most populated, with large industrial cities. The other countries are more mountainous and sparsely populated, but for a few industrial areas.

FACE THE FACTS…

❖ The land
The UK's highest point is Ben Nevis (1343 m) and its longest river is the Severn (320 km). Ireland's highest point is Carrauntoohil (1040 m); longest river: the Shannon (386 km).

❖ Climate
The British Isles and Ireland lie quite far north, but their climate is kept mild (and wet) by the warm Gulf Stream current flowing across the Atlantic from the Caribbean. Ireland, Wales and western Scotland are especially mild and wet.

❖ Population
The UK's population is 59.5 m; Ireland's is 3.7 m.

❖ Capitals
England's, London, with 7.3 million people; Wales's, Cardiff; Scotland's, Edinburgh; Northern Ireland's, Belfast; Ireland's, Dublin.

❖ Natural resources
Coal and iron ore mining has dwindled in the UK, but huge quantities of oil and natural gas come from under the North Sea.

❖ Farming
England is intensively farmed, especially in the southeast where wheat, barley, rape, sugar beet and vegetables are grown. In the moister north and west of Britain, cows are reared in the lowlands and sheep on the hills.

❖ Fishing
The UK has about 11,000 fishing boats.

❖ Industry and commerce
The UK is a leading industrial country, but manufacturing is not as dominant as it was. Light engineering and car-making are important, but over half the labour force works in financial and service industries. In Ireland, industry has grown, and brewing, food-processing and textiles have been joined by chemicals and electronics.

❖ Government
The UK has a queen but the country is run by a government formed from the party with a majority in the elected House of Commons, led by a prime minister. Ireland (Eire) is a republic but the president has little power, and the country is run by the taoiseach (prime minister) and a cabinet nominated by the Dáil (House).

❖ Religion
Anglican Protestantism in the UK, Roman Catholicism in Eire.

❖ Language
Most people speak English, but Scotland, Wales and Ireland have their own languages.

❖ Currency
The UK's currency is the pound Sterling; Ireland's is the Euro.

❖ Sport
Cricket, rugby and football are the most popular.

Stag
The Highlands of Scotland are wild, mountainous and often spectacularly beautiful. Their wildlife includes red deer and the capercaillie, a giant turkey-like bird capable of making extraordinary noises.

Cow country
Cows have been valued in Ireland since ancient times. They were the subject of mythical, epic tales in which heroes fought to win prized cattle. Now they are at the heart of a major dairy industry.

Old Clyde
In the past, northern cities thrived on heavy industry, and Glasgow's famous Clyde shipyards once rang to the sound of great ocean liners being built. But all over the country these industries have declined in the face of foreign competition.

Edinburgh Castle
Edinburgh is the capital of Scotland and home of the new Scottish Parliament. It is a spectacular city with two distinct parts. On the Castle Mound there is the Old Town with its tall dark granite houses. To the north is the elegant New Town built in the 18th century.

SHETLAND ISLANDS

Lerwick

ORKNEY ISLANDS

John o'Groats

Aberdeen
Dee

Dundee

Firth of Forth

Inverness

Moray Firth

Spey

Tay

SCOTLAND

GRAMPIAN MOUNTAINS

Perth

Forth

EDINBURGH

Clyde

NORTH WEST HIGHLANDS

Ben Nevis △ 1343 m
Loch Ness

Loch Lomond

Glasgow

Ayr

Arran

Mull

Islay

Skye

Rhum

North Minch

INNER HEBRIDES

OUTER HEBRIDES

Lewis

North Uist

South Uist

NORTH CHANNEL

Londonderry

NORTHERN IRELAND

Lough Neagh

BELFAST

Donegal

Donegal Bay

ATLANTIC OCEAN

Newcastle upon Tyne

Tyne

Sunderland

Middlesbrough

Carlisle

CUMBRIAN MOUNTAINS

SOUTHERN UPLANDS

Tweed

PENNINES

UNITED

NORTH SEA

ATLANTIC OCEAN

SCOTLAND

UNITED KINGDOM

IRELAND

WALES ENGLAND

NORTH SEA

ENGLISH CHANNEL

DENMARK

NETHERLANDS

BELGIUM GERMANY

LUXEMBOURG

FRANCE

SWITZERLAND

AUSTRIA HUNGARY

SLOVENIA

CROATIA BOSNIA HERZEGOVINA

YUGOSLAVIA

ITALY

GREECE

ALBANIA

MEDITERRANEAN SEA

SPAIN

POLAND

CZECH REP.

SLOVAKIA

ROMANIA

Miles
0   25   50   75   100

Kilometres
0   25   50   75   100   125   150

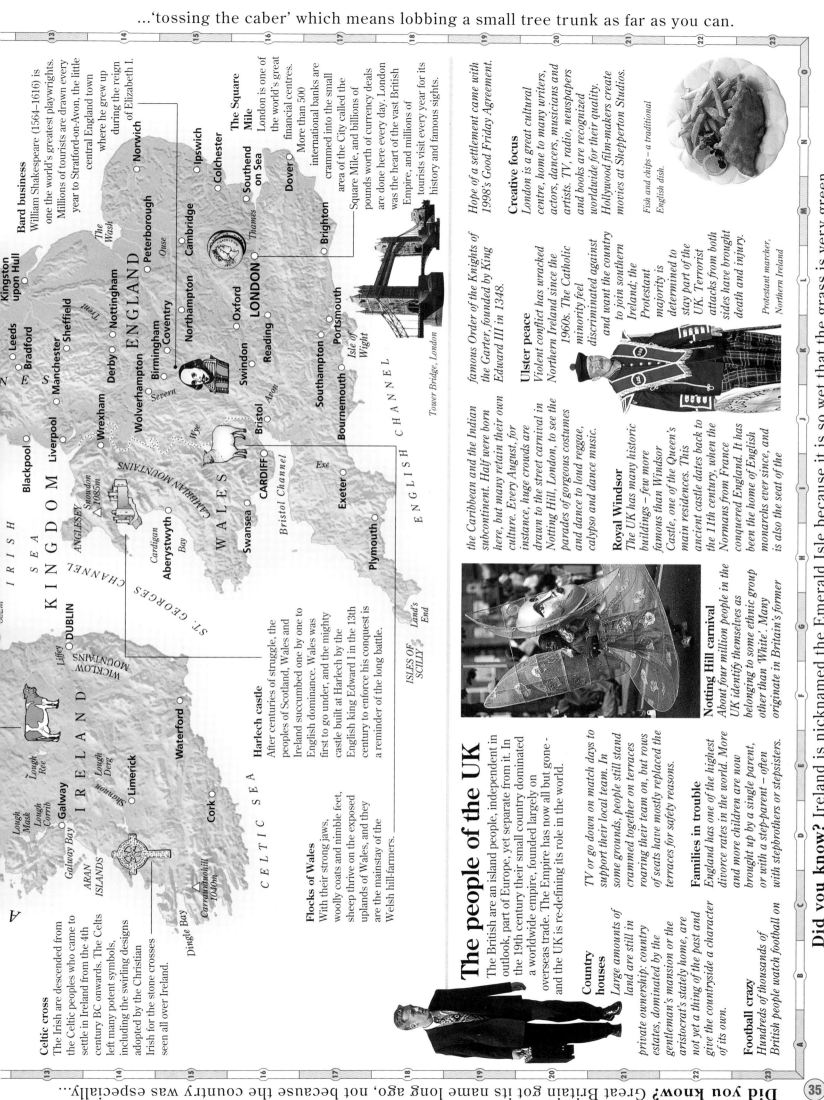

Celtic cross
The Irish are descended from the Celtic peoples who came to settle in Ireland from the 4th century BC onwards. The Celts left many potent symbols, including the swirling designs adopted by the Christian Irish for the stone crosses seen all over Ireland.

Bard business
William Shakespeare (1564–1616) is one of the world's greatest playwrights. Millions of tourists are drawn every year to Stratford-on-Avon, the little central England town where he grew up during the reign of Elizabeth I.

The Square Mile
London is one of the world's great financial centres. More than 500 international banks are crammed into the small area of the City called the Square Mile, and billions of pounds worth of currency deals are done here every day. London was the heart of the vast British Empire, and millions of tourists visit every year for its history and famous sights.

Tower Bridge, London

Hope of a settlement came with 1998's Good Friday Agreement.

Creative focus
London is a great cultural centre, home to many writers, actors, dancers, musicians and artists. TV, radio, newspapers and books are recognized worldwide for their quality. Hollywood film-makers create movies at Shepperton Studios.

Fish and chips – a traditional English dish.

famous Order of the Knights of the Garter, founded by King Edward III in 1348.

Ulster peace
Violent conflict has wracked Northern Ireland since the 1960s. The Catholic minority feel discriminated against and want the country to join southern Ireland; the Protestant majority is determined to stay part of the UK. Terrorist attacks from both sides have brought death and injury.

Protestant marcher, Northern Ireland

the Caribbean and the Indian subcontinent. Half were born here, but many retain their own culture. Every August, for instance, huge crowds are drawn to the street carnival in Notting Hill, London, to see the parades of gorgeous costumes and dance to loud reggae, calypso and dance music.

Royal Windsor
The UK has many historic buildings – few more famous than Windsor Castle, one of the Queen's main residences. This ancient castle dates back to the 11th century, when the Normans from France conquered England. It has been the home of English monarchs ever since, and is also the seat of the

Notting Hill carnival
About four million people in the UK identify themselves as belonging to some ethnic group other than 'White'. Many originate in Britain's former

The people of the UK

The British are an island people, independent in outlook, part of Europe, yet separate from it. In the 19th century their small country dominated a worldwide empire, founded largely on overseas trade. The Empire has now all but gone - and the UK is re-defining its role in the world.

Country houses
Large amounts of land are still in private ownership: country estates, dominated by the gentleman's mansion or the aristocrat's stately home, are not yet a thing of the past and give the countryside a character of its own.

Football crazy
Hundreds of thousands of British people watch football on

TV or go down on match days to support their local team. In some grounds, people still stand crammed together on terraces roaring their team on, but rows of seats have mostly replaced the terraces for safety reasons.

Families in trouble
England has one of the highest divorce rates in the world. More and more children are now brought up by a single parent, or with a step-parent – often with stepbrothers or stepsisters.

Harlech castle
After centuries of struggle, the peoples of Scotland, Wales and Ireland succumbed one by one to English dominance. Wales was first to go under, and the mighty castle built at Harlech by the English king Edward I in the 13th century to enforce his conquest is a reminder of the long battle.

Flocks of Wales
With their strong jaws, woolly coats and nimble feet, sheep thrive on the exposed uplands of Wales, and they are the mainstay of the Welsh hill-farmers.

Map labels:
IRELAND
DUBLIN
Liffey
WICKLOW MOUNTAINS
Galway Bay · Galway
Lough Corrib
Lough Mask
Lough Ree
Lough Derg
Shannon
ARAN ISLANDS
Limerick
Waterford
Cork
Carrantuohill 1040m
Dingle Bay
CELTIC SEA
ST. GEORGE'S CHANNEL

IRISH SEA
KINGDOM
ANGLESEY
Snowdon △ 1085m
CAMBRIAN MOUNTAINS
Aberystwyth
Cardigan Bay
WALES
Swansea
CARDIFF
Bristol Channel
Wrexham
Wolverhampton
Birmingham
Coventry
Severn
Wye
Exe
Avon
Bristol
Exeter
Plymouth
Land's End
ISLES OF SCILLY
ENGLISH CHANNEL
Bournemouth
Southampton
Portsmouth
Isle of Wight

Blackpool
Liverpool
Manchester
Bradford
Leeds
Sheffield
Derby
Nottingham
ENGLAND
Trent
Northampton
Oxford
Swindon
Reading
LONDON
Thames
Brighton
Southend on Sea
Dover
Colchester
Ipswich
Norwich
The Wash
Ouse
Peterborough
Cambridge
Kingston upon Hull

Did you know? Great Britain got its name long ago, not because the country was especially...

35

Did you know? The word 'denim' comes from the town of Nîmes – *de Nîmes* means 'from Nîmes'.

FACE THE FACTS...

❖ The land
France's highest mountain is Mont Blanc (4807 m), which is also the highest mountain in Europe. Its longest river is the Loire (1005 km).

❖ Climate
There are three different climatic regions – the Atlantic northwest, which is mild but damp; the continental east which has hot summers and stormy winters; and the Mediterranean south which has mild winters and hot, dry summers when forest fires are common.

❖ Population
The population of France is 58.5 million, one-sixth of whom live in Paris.

❖ Capital
France's capital is Paris, visited by more tourists each year than any other city in the world.

❖ Natural resources
France is not especially rich in mineral resources, and coal and iron, once plentiful, are now depleted.

❖ Farming
France is Europe's biggest food producer apart from Russia. Wheat and sugar beet are grown in the north and west of the country, while grapes and other fruit are grown widely in the south. In summer, many fields are yellow with sunflowers, which provide food for livestock and oil for cooking.

❖ Industry and commerce
The leading French industries are engineering, including carmaking, telecommunications and aerospace, textiles, chemicals, nuclear power and steel. France is also a world leader in luxury goods such as cosmetics, perfumes, fine wines and fashion.

❖ Government
France was the world's first modern republic. It is headed by a president, but run by a prime minisister and ministers elected to parliament.

❖ Religion
90 per cent of French people are Roman Catholic.

❖ Currency
The Franc.

❖ Sport
The most popular sport is football, but the game of boules (rather like bowls but with smaller balls) is a traditional game played throughout France. It is often played in the local square of a town or village.

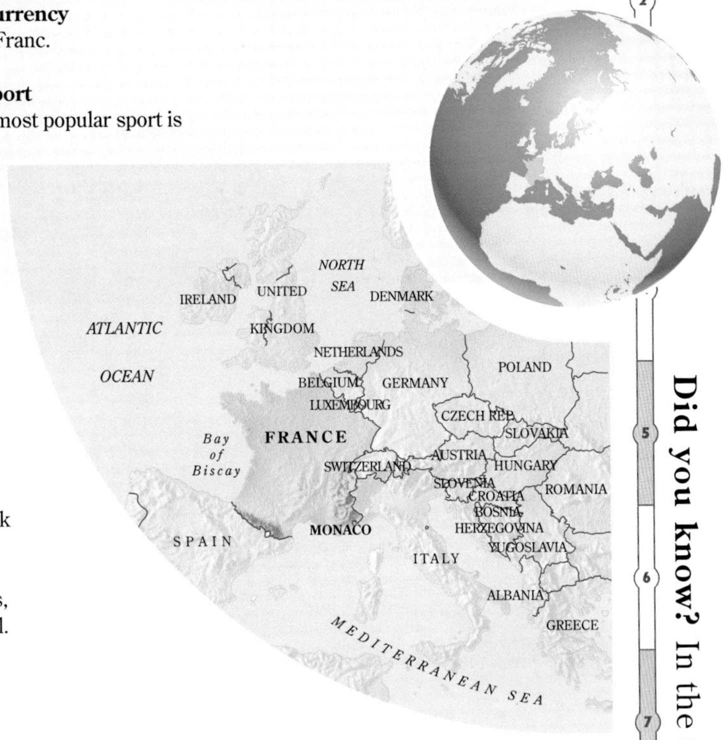

ATLANTIC
OCEAN
IRELAND
UNITED KINGDOM
NORTH SEA
DENMARK
NETHERLANDS
BELGIUM
LUXEMBOURG
GERMANY
POLAND
CZECH REP.
SLOVAKIA
FRANCE
Bay of Biscay
SWITZERLAND
AUSTRIA
HUNGARY
SLOVENIA
CROATIA
ROMANIA
BOSNIA-HERZEGOVINA
YUGOSLAVIA
SPAIN
MONACO
ITALY
ALBANIA
GREECE
MEDITERRANEAN SEA

France

Stretching from the rugged Atlantic coast of Brittany to the warm Cote d'Azur on the Mediterranean, France is western Europe's biggest country. Much of it is still rural, with sleepy old towns, villages and farmhouses scattered through a countryside that has changed little in a hundred years. But its cities, famous for their sophisticated culture, provide a base for so much industry that France is the world's fourth largest industrial power after the USA, Japan and Germany.

Nuclear power
With limited coal and oil supplies, France has made the most of other power sources. It now has one of the world's biggest nuclear power industries and 75 per cent of the country's energy is nuclear.

Notre Dame
Paris is a historic city, with many famous buildings, including the 300-m high Eiffel Tower and cathedral of Notre Dame, where the great French writer Victor Hugo (1802–85) set his story about Quasimodo, 'the hunchback of Notre Dame'. Paris was the centre of the French Revolution of the 1790s, and Napoleon's capital.

Miles 0 25 50 75 100 125
Kilometres 0 50 100 150 200
ENGLISH CHANNEL
Calais
Dunkerque
Boulogne
BELGIUM
Somme
Dieppe
Amiens
Cherbourg
Bay of the Seine
Le Havre
Rouen
Beauvais
LUXEMBOURG
Reims
Meuse
Metz
GERMANY
Caen
Seine
Gulf of St. Malo
PARIS
Marne
Moselle
Strasbourg
Brest
St.-Malo
MONTS D'ARREE
MONTAGNE NOIRE
COLLINES DE NORMANDIE
Seine
VOSGES
Rhine
Rennes
Le Mans
Orléans
Mulhouse
Loir
Saône
Angers
Loire
Tours
Nantes
Loire
Dijon
Besançon
Cher
JURA
Poitiers
F R A N C E

High-speed train
France has some of the fastest trains in the world. Known as TGVs (*Train à Grand Vitesse*), these superfast electric trains run on specially built tracks at speeds of up to 515 km/h.

Breton stone circle
The province of Brittany in the west is the home of the Bretons, a Celtic people who try to preservetheir own language and traditions. Stone circles testify to the antiquity of their culture.

Did you know? There are some 400 different types of French cheese.

Did you know? In the south they greet each other by...

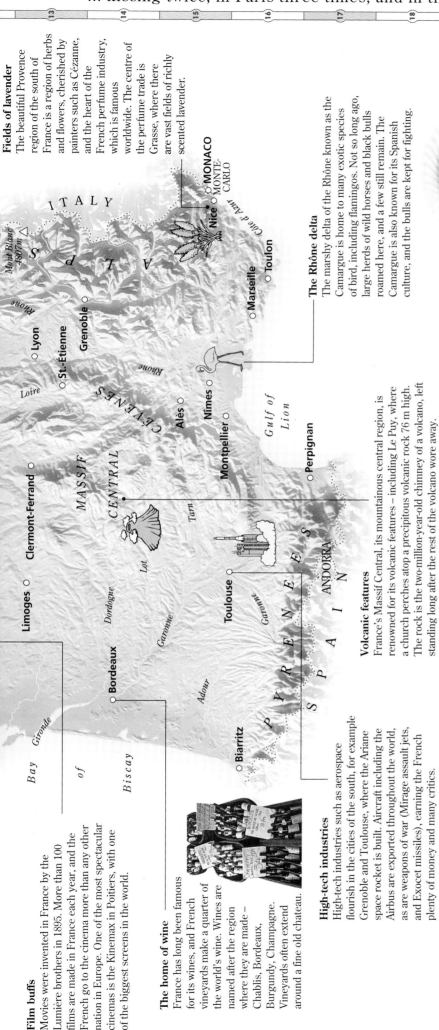

Fields of lavender

The beautiful Provence region of the south of France is a region of herbs and flowers, cherished by painters such as Cézanne, and the heart of the French perfume industry, which is famous worldwide. The centre of the perfume trade is Grasse, where there are vast fields of richly scented lavender.

MONACO
MONTE-CARLO

Nice

Côte d'Azur

ITALY

Mont Blanc
4807m

A L P S

Rhône

Lyon

St-Étienne

Grenoble

Marseille

Toulon

The Rhône delta

The marshy delta of the Rhône known as the Camargue is home to many exotic species of bird, including flamingos. Not so long ago, large herds of wild horses and black bulls roamed here, and a few still remain. The Camargue is also known for its Spanish culture, and the bulls are kept for fighting.

Loire

Rhône

Nîmes

Alès

Montpellier

Gulf of Lion

Perpignan

C É V E N N E S

MASSIF
CENTRAL

Clermont-Ferrand

Limoges

Tarn

Lot

Dordogne

Garonne

Toulouse

Garonne

Adour

Bordeaux

P Y R E N E E S

ANDORRA

S P A I N

Biarritz

Bay

of

Biscay

Girande

Gironde

Volcanic features

France's Massif Central, its mountainous central region, is renowned for its volcanic features – including Le Puy, where a church perches atop a precipitous volcanic rock 76 m high. The rock is the two-million-year-old chimney of a volcano, left standing long after the rest of the volcano wore away.

High-tech industries

High-tech industries such as aerospace flourish in the cities of the south, for example Grenoble and Toulouse, where the Ariane space rocket is built. Aircraft including the Airbus are exported throughout the world, as are weapons of war (Mirage assault jets, and Exocet missiles), earning the French plenty of money and many critics.

Film buffs

Movies were invented in France by the Lumière brothers in 1895. More than 100 films are made in France each year, and the French go to the cinema more than any other nation in Europe. One of the most spectacular cinemas is the Kinemax in Poitiers, with one of the biggest screens in the world.

The home of wine

France has long been famous for its wines, and French vineyards make a quarter of the world's wine. Wines are named after the region where they are made – Chablis, Bordeaux, Burgundy, Champagne. Vineyards often extend around a fine old chateau.

Food lovers

The French love good food. In the past, every town had a market for high quality fruit and vegetables, delicatessens for fine cheeses, charcuteries for cooked meats, patisseries for cakes and pastries, and much more besides. Now many of these shops are collected together in giant hypermarkets out of town, but the good food is still there.

À la carte

France is famous for its cooking, and French cuisine has often been regarded as the very best luxury food. In France, top chefs can often be as famous as film stars.

Le fromage

French beef cattle such as the Charolais and Limousin are world famous, but France's real speciality is cheese. There are hundreds of different delicious French cheeses, some made from cow's milk, like Brie and Camembert, and some from sheep's milk, like Roquefort.

Tour de France

The annual Tour de France is one of the world's most famous cycling races. It lasts 26 days, during which cyclists have to power their way up through most of France's mountain regions and some neighbouring countries, ending up in Paris.

At the end of each day, the leader is presented with le maillot jaune (the yellow jersey).

Marseilles in the south has become home to many people from North Africa – the presence here of a large immigrant population has fuelled racial tensions.

Le car

France has one of the world's largest motor industries, and, in the past, at least, French cars – including Renault, Citroën and Peugeot – were known for their stylish, distinctive design.

Café society

Nothing typifies the French way of life better than the café, where people while away the hours, drinking strong coffee, talking earnestly and watching the world go by.

Algerian French

France has an immigrant population of 3.5 million – mostly from its former colonies in North Africa (Algeria, Tunisia and Morocco) and West Africa. The port of

The French

The French are proud that they have given the world so many of the good things of life: delicious food, fine wine, high fashion; and they are great talkers, meeters and greeters.

Paris fashion show

Paris is a sophisticated city famous for its culture and design, summed up by the

word 'chic'. Each spring, leading fashion designers come to Paris to present their latest collections.

Did you know? Roses are planted in vineyards – the health of the rose tells the farmer the health of the vines.

Did you know? People in France use more than 1 kilogram of mustard per year each.

37

The Low Countries

Belgium, the Netherlands and Luxembourg are together aptly known as the Low Countries. Except for the Ardennes hills in southern Belgium, they are almost all low-lying and much of the Netherlands is actually below sea-level, only protected from flooding by banks called dykes. They are small but very densely populated countries, where large numbers of people live in old market towns and big industrial cities.

FACE THE FACTS…

❖ The land
Belgium's highest hill is Botrange (694 m); the highest in the Netherlands is Vaalser Berg (321 m); Luxembourg's is Buurgplatz (559 m). Belgium's longest river is the Meuse (901 km); the longest river in the Netherlands is the Rhine (1320 km).

❖ Climate
The climate is temperate, with mild winters and short summers.

❖ Population
Belgium 10.2 m people, more than 96 per cent of whom live in towns; the Netherlands has 15.8 m; and Luxembourg has 432,000.

❖ Capitals
See the map.

❖ Resources
Belgium's coal reserves have now all but run out, but the Netherlands remains one of Europe's biggest producers of natural gas.

❖ Farming
Belgium and the Netherlands are both intensively farmed. The Netherlands is famous for dairy produce, greenhouse vegetables, cut flowers, bulbs and seeds. Belgium has many dairy farms too; flax is grown in the north, plus cereals, sugarbeet, potatoes and Brussels sprouts.

❖ Fishing
Herring, mackerel and cod in the North Sea. Inshore fishermen gather mussels, oysters, crabs and other shellfish.

❖ Industry & commerce
All three countries are heavily industrialized. Belgium and Luxembourg are known for steel, while Belgium is an important textile exporter. The Netherlands has large shipyards, also major electronics and chemicals industries. Some of the world's biggest companies, including Shell and Philips, are Dutch.

❖ Government
Belgium and the Netherlands both have monarchs as their heads of state, while Luxembourg has a Grand Duke, but all are run by elected parliaments.

❖ Language
In the Netherlands they speak Dutch; in Luxembourg the official language is Letzeburgish but most people also speak French and German; in Belgium, people speak Dutch, French or German.

❖ Religion
Most Belgians are Roman Catholic; a third of the Dutch are Roman Catholic, a third are Protestant and a third hold other beliefs.

❖ Sport
National sports: football, cycling and skating.

❖ Currency
The euro is now the sole official currency in the Low Countries.

Venice of the North
Amsterdam is an attractive old city, with more than 160 canals, created when the city grew rich and expanded across marshy ground in the 1600s. The beautiful, narrow brick merchants' houses that line the canals date from this time and are built on wooden piles, driven into solid ground way below the marshland. Today, the city is a magnet for young people, who like its bustle and relaxed way of life.

European Gateway
Linked to the sea by a short channel, Rotterdam is one of the world's busiest ports, handling almost a million tonnes of goods a day from all over the world. Goods are transferred to barges to be taken by canal and via the great Rhine and Maas rivers far into Europe.

The Afsluitdijk
The Afsluitdijk is an embankment over 30 km long. Completed in 1932, it turned an inland sea called the Zuyder Zee into a vast lake called the Ijsselmeer. A large part of the lake has now been drained to create land for farming and houses, adding 6 per cent (1200 sq km) to the land area of the Netherlands.

Land from the water
Well over a third of the Netherlands is polders – land once covered by the sea, lakes or marsh and now pumped dry and protected by dykes. The windmills scattered across the landscape bear witness to the long battle to keep the water at bay. Nowadays, though, the pumping is done not by windmills but by electric and diesel pumps.

Map labels
NORWAY, SWEDEN, DENMARK, UNITED KINGDOM, IRELAND, NORTH SEA, ATLANTIC OCEAN, NETHERLANDS, BELGIUM, LUXEMBOURG, FRANCE, GERMANY, SWITZERLAND, ITALY, AUSTRIA, CZECH REP., POLAND, LITHUANIA, RUSSIA, BELARUS, UKRAINE, SLOVAKIA, HUNGARY, SLOVENIA, CROATIA, BOSNIA, HERZEGOVINA, YUGOSLAVIA, ROMANIA, MOLDOVA, BULGARIA, MACEDONIA, ALBANIA, GREECE, TURKEY, BLACK SEA, MEDITERRANEAN SEA

WEST FRISIAN ISLANDS, Groningen, Enschede, Apeldoorn, Arnhem, Rhine, Nijmegen, Waal, Meuse, Lek, Utrecht, Amersfoort, AMSTERDAM, Markermeer, Ijsselmeer, Waddenzee, Leiden, Haarlem, The Hague, Rotterdam, Dordrecht, NETHERLANDS, Maas

Miles 0 10 20 30 40 50
Kilometres 0 20 40 60 80

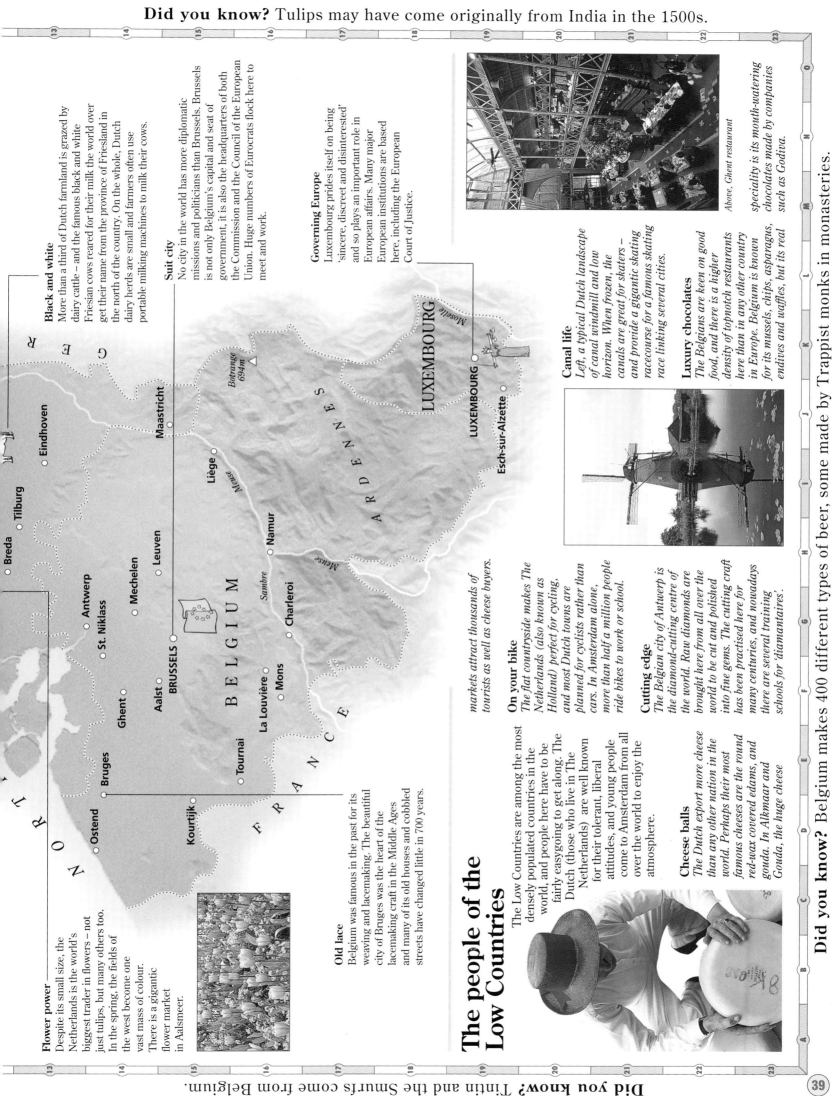

The people of the Low Countries

The Low Countries are among the most densely populated countries in the world, and people here have to be fairly easygoing to get along. The Dutch (those who live in The Netherlands) are well known for their tolerant, liberal attitudes, and young people come to Amsterdam from all over the world to enjoy the atmosphere.

Cheese balls
The Dutch export more cheese than any other nation in the world. Perhaps their most famous cheeses are the round red-wax covered edams, and gouda. In Alkmaar and Gouda, the huge cheese markets attract thousands of tourists as well as cheese buyers.

On your bike
The flat countryside makes The Netherlands (also known as Holland) perfect for cycling, and most Dutch towns are planned for cyclists rather than cars. In Amsterdam alone, more than half a million people ride bikes to work or school.

Cutting edge
The Belgian city of Antwerp is the diamond-cutting centre of the world. Raw diamonds are brought here from all over the world to be cut and polished into fine gems. The cutting craft has been practised here for many centuries, and nowadays there are several training schools for 'diamantaires'.

Flower power
Despite its small size, the Netherlands is the world's biggest trader in flowers – not just tulips, but many others too. In the spring, the fields of the west become one vast mass of colour. There is a gigantic flower market in Aalsmeer.

Old lace
Belgium was famous in the past for its weaving and lacemaking. The beautiful city of Bruges was the heart of the lacemaking craft in the Middle Ages and many of its old houses and cobbled streets have changed little in 700 years.

Black and white
More than a third of Dutch farmland is grazed by dairy cattle – and the famous black and white Friesian cows reared for their milk the world over get their name from the province of Friesland in the north of the country. On the whole, Dutch dairy herds are small and farmers often use portable milking machines to milk their cows.

Suit city
No city in the world has more diplomatic missions and politicians than Brussels. Brussels is not only Belgium's capital and seat of government, it is also the headquarters of both the Commission and the Council of the European Union. Huge numbers of Eurocrats flock here to meet and work.

Governing Europe
Luxembourg prides itself on being 'sincere, discreet and disinterested' and so plays an important role in European affairs. Many major European institutions are based here, including the European Court of Justice.

Canal life
Left, a typical Dutch landscape of canal windmill and low horizon. When frozen, the canals are great for skaters – and provide a gigantic skating racecourse for a famous skating race linking several cities.

Luxury chocolates
The Belgians are keen on good food, and there is a higher density of topnotch restaurants here than in any other country in Europe. Belgium is known for its mussels, chips, asparagus, endives and waffles, but its real speciality is its mouth-watering chocolates made by companies such as Godiva.

Above, Ghent restaurant

Map labels:
- Breda
- Tilburg
- Eindhoven
- Maastricht
- Antwerp
- St. Niklass
- Mechelen
- Leuven
- Ghent
- Aalst
- BRUSSELS
- BELGIUM
- Bruges
- Ostend
- Kourtijk
- Tournai
- La Louvière
- Mons
- Charleroi
- Namur
- Liège
- Sambre
- Meuse
- Meuse
- ARDENNES
- Botrange 694m
- LUXEMBOURG
- LUXEMBOURG
- Esch-sur-Alzette
- Moselle
- FRANCE
- GERMANY

Did you know? Belgium makes 400 different types of beer, some made by Trappist monks in monasteries.

Germany, Austria and Switzerland

Lying at the heart of the continent, Europe's three German-speaking nations – Germany, Switzerland and Austria – are among the world's richest. Germany is by far the largest of the three. Switzerland and Austria are small but beautiful, mountainous countries.

FACE THE FACTS...

❖ The land
The highest mountain in Germany is Zugspitze (2963 m), but Austria has Grössglockner (3801 m) and Switzerland has Dufourspitze on Monte Rosa (4638 m). The longest river is the Danube 2859 km long, but the Rhine is also long at 1320 km.

❖ Climate
Most of Germany has a mild temperate climate with cool winters and warm summers. But winters in the Alps can be severe.

❖ Population
Germany 82.1 m; Austria 8 m; Switzerland 7.1 m.

❖ Capitals
Germany's capital is Berlin, once divided in two by the Berlin Wall but now one city; Austria's capital is Vienna; Switzerland's is Berne.

❖ Natural resources
Germany has extensive coal, brown coal and salt resources, but all three countries rely heavily on imports for most other things.

❖ Forestry
Almost a third of Germany and Austria is covered in forests, and both are major exporters of timber.

❖ Farming
Many farms are small, family-run businesses, yet all three countries manage to be almost self-sufficient in food. Major crops in Germany are cereals and sugarbeet. Cows and pigs are plentiful. The Alps are famous for their rich pastures.

❖ Industry and commerce
The world's third biggest manufacturing nation after the USA and Japan, Germany is famous for technology and quality products. Switzerland has grown rich from banking and making small valuable things such as precision instruments, but also has a major chemical industry.

❖ Government
Germany, Switzerland and Austria are federal republics. This means that although the federal government runs the country, the various regions – Länder in Germany and cantons in Switzerland – have considerable power.

❖ Language
Germany and Austria are German-speaking. In the north of Switzerland, most speak a form of German; in the west French; in the south Italian; and in the east a few speak Romansch.

❖ Religion
Most Austrians are Roman Catholics; in Germany and Switzerland, just under half the population are Roman Catholic and half Protestant.

❖ Sport
Skiing is the national sport of Switzerland and Austria. In Germany, football is by far the biggest sport.

❖ Currency
The euro is the currency of Austria and Germany. Switzerland uses the Swiss franc.

Window on the world
Hamburg has been a great port since before the Middle Ages. It remains one of the world's largest and busiest ports, and one of Germany's leading cities.

Steel country
The Ruhr valley was for a long time Germany's industrial heartland. Scores of coal mines fed huge steelworks, and the steelworks supplied massive engineering firms. Now the easily accessible coal has been exhausted, and many mines and steelworks have closed. But the Ruhr remains one of the world's most important industrial regions.

Soviet war memorial near the Brandenburg Gate, Berlin

Gateway to unity
After World War II, Germany was split in two parts – West and East Germany. East Germany was a strictly communist country, and the old German capital of Berlin, cut off from the West, was divided by a high wall topped with barbed wire and machine gun posts. But on October 3, 1990, Germany was reunited, and the Berlin Wall was demolished by cheering Berliners. Berlin became capital again and traffic flowed freely through the city's famous Brandenburg Gate.

Rye smile
Much of north Germany is flat heath and marsh, but there is rich farmland too, and here cereals are grown extensively. This part of Germany is famous for its rye bread.

POLAND

Baltic Sea

Rügen

Klimes Hüff

Oder

BERLIN

Müritz See

Elbe

Leipzig

Dresden

Magdeburg

Halle

Mecklenburger Bucht

Elbe

Aller

Hamburg

Fehmarn

Kieler Bucht

Weser

Bremen

Hanover

Bielefeld

Weser

DENMARK

Sylt

NORTH FRISIAN ISLANDS

NORTH SEA

EAST FRISIAN ISLANDS

Ems

Gelsenkirchen

Dortmund

Bochum

Duisburg

Essen

Düsseldorf

Wuppertal

Cologne

Rhine

NETHERLANDS

GERMANY

ATLANTIC OCEAN

IRELAND

UNITED KINGDOM

NORTH SEA

NETHERLANDS

BELGIUM

LUXEMBOURG

FRANCE

NORWAY

SWEDEN

DENMARK

BALTIC SEA

POLAND

BELARUS

UKRAINE

GERMANY

CZECH REP.

SLOVAKIA

MOLDOVA

SWITZERLAND

AUSTRIA

SLOVENIA

HUNGARY

ROMANIA

CROATIA

BOSNIA HERZEGOVINA

YUGOSLAVIA

BULGARIA

BLACK SEA

TURKEY

ITALY

MACEDONIA

ALBANIA

GREECE

MEDITERRANEAN SEA

Did you know? On their first day of school, German children get a big paper cone full of sweets called a *Schultüte*.

Schubert

Vienna Opera House
When the Austrian Empire still thrived, back in the 19th century, Vienna was the music capital of Europe. Although some of the city's glory has faded, it still boasts one of the world's great opera houses.

Auto power
Germany is one of the great carmaking nations of the world. The very first petrol driven car was made by Karl Benz here in Germany back in 1885. Nowadays only the USA and Japan make more cars.

Wurst is best
Every region in Germany has its own special foods, but things like pretzels, wurst (sausages) and sauerkraut (pickled cabbage) are popular all over the country. Among the most famous German wines is Riesling, but the national drink is beer, and every October a huge beer festival is held in Munich.

...laws and people began recycling rubbish. Most houses now have three separate dustbins for different types of waste. But East Germany was one of the most polluted countries in the world, and this area is only gradually being cleaned up.

Green country
When thousands of trees began to die from acid rain in their beloved Black Forest, many West Germans began to worry about the damage humans were doing to the environment. The country introduced tough anti-pollution

Kaffee and Kuchen
Vienna is famous for its coffee houses. Here the Viennese meet or sit and read for hours while drinking coffee and choosing from a huge selection of delicious cakes and pastries.

Walking
Walking, especially in southern Germany and the Alps, is the favourite pastime for Germans, Austrians and the Swiss.

Below, winter is a great time for children in the Alps.

high-tech industries and carmaking are booming, and the countryside is pleasant with the Alps nearby.

New arrivals
In the 1960s, the growing German economy needed extra workers, and thousands of people came here from Turkey and Eastern Europe. Discrimination has made life difficult for these newcomers and many have been refused citizenship. In the 1990s, a further million Eastern Europeans arrived and 8.9 per cent of Germans are now foreign born.

Bankers
Because Switzerland is so stable politically – and because its banking laws guarantee secrecy – many rich people from all over the world put their money in Swiss banks. No one knows just how much money is held in the banks in Zurich, but it is certainly a great deal.

Skis and chalets
Hundreds of thousands of tourists are drawn to the spectacular scenery of the Alps every year. In winter, skiers come for some of the best skiing in the world.

Swiss time
With few mineral resources, Switzerland has made the most of a skilled labour force to build up industries based on high-value, lightweight products such as medicines, chocolate and watches.

Safe haven
For centuries, Switzerland has been a 'neutral' country, staying aloof from conflicts. This is why organizations such as the Red Cross and the World Health Organization have made their base in Geneva. The Red Cross emblem is a reverse image of the Swiss flag.

The Germans

Germans have a reputation for being disciplined and efficient, and their working day starts early. But they earn high wages and take long holidays. Their cities are increasingly relaxed, cultured places and their young spend money, just as elsewhere in Western Europe, on looking good.

Hot cheese
One of the best-known Swiss dishes is fondue. For a cheese fondue, bread impaled on long forks is dipped into a scalding bowl of melted Gruyère or Emmental cheese mixed with wine, garlic, pepper and kirsch (cherry liqueur).

Clean living
Fed up with the grime and unemployment of the old industrial centres, many Germans have moved to cities in the south of the country, such as Stuttgart and Munich. Here

Map labels: SLOVAKIA, HUNGARY, Neusiedler Lake, VIENNA, St Pölten, Graz, Danube, Linz, Wels, Enns, AUSTRIA, Salzburg, Mur, SLOVENIA, Klagenfurt, Villach, Drava, Großglockner 3811m, Inn, Munich, Innsbruck, Zugspitze 2963m, Lech, ITALY, CZECH REPUBLIC, Nuremberg, Main, Danube, Stuttgart, Frankfurt am Main, Karlsruhe, Mannheim, Rhine, Lake Constance, Winterthur, St Gallen, Zurich, Lucerne, SWITZERLAND, Basel, Rhine, LUXEMBOURG, Moselle, Saar, FRANCE, Biel, BERNE, Lausanne, Lake Geneva, Geneva, Rhône, Monte Rosa 4638m, Matterhorn 4478m, SLOVENIA

Miles / Kilometres scale: 0 25 50 75 100 / 0 50 100 150

FACE THE FACTS...

❖ **The land**
Norway's highest point is Glittertind (2472 m); Sweden's is Kebnekaise (2123 m); Finland's is Mt Haltiatunturi (1324 m) and Denmark's is Yding Skovhøj (173 m). The longest river is Finland's Kemi (547 km).

❖ **Climate**
Scandinavia is generally quite cool, even in summer. Winters inland can be very cold indeed, with the northern Baltic freezing over.

❖ **Population**
Norway 4.4 m; Sweden 8.8 m, 85 per cent of whom live in the south; Finland 5.1 m; Denmark 5.3m.

❖ **Capitals**
See the map.

❖ **Resources**
Norway is Europe's largest producer of oil and natural gas.

Sweden has abundant iron ore, copper and silver and produces 80 per cent of Europe's uranium.

❖ **Farming**
Apart from Denmark, only a small proportion of Scandinavia can be farmed, and much of the farmland is pasture. Nearly all of Denmark, however, is intensively farmed.

❖ **Fishing**
Norwegian fishing boats venture far out across the North Atlantic to catch the shoals of herring and cod brought in by the Gulf Stream. The country catches nearly 2.6 million tonnes of fish a year – more than any other European country except for Russia.

❖ **Forestry**
Norway, Sweden and Finland are covered with swathes of pine forest and have large-scale timber industries. Finland is one of the world's biggest paper makers.

❖ **Industry & commerce**
Sweden is renowned for its high-quality engineering, with car- and aircraft-makers such as Saab and Volvo. Sweden is also known, along with Finland, for its glass and ceramics. Denmark specializes in high-tech products and food-processing.

❖ **Government**
All of the Scandinavian countries except Finland have a king or a queen, and they are run by an elected government headed by a prime minister. Since 1993, the Sami, or Lapp people, have had their own council in Sweden called the Sameting.

❖ **Religion**
Most people in Scandinavia are Protestant Christians.

❖ **Language**
Each country has its own language. The Sami people also have their own language.

❖ **Sport**
Cross-country skiing is Norway's national sport; tennis is popular in Sweden; Danes enjoy riding, cycling, and windsurfing; the Finns are great at ice hockey.

Wooden house
Over half of Sweden is covered by forest, so it is not surprising that many Swedish homes are built of wood. Because the trees grew slowly, the wood is dense and good for building.

Lapland
In the far north live the Lapp or Sami people. In the past, the Sami were reindeer herders who lived in reindeer-skin tents. Now, half the Sami live in permanent farms and most of the rest live on the coast, fishing, farming and mining.

Logging in
Logging is very big business in Scandinavia and it produces a huge proportion of Europe's wood, paper and furniture. But so many trees are being cut down that even the vast northern forests are dwindling – which is why the Swedes are trying to develop more environmentally friendly forestry techniques.

Right, Danish traditional costume - and drinking horn.

Scandinavia

The countries of Scandinavia are among the most northerly inhabited in the world, reaching far into the Arctic circle. Norway and Sweden are rugged and mountainous, while Finland is a land of forests and lakes. Only Denmark is flat and mild. Yet the small populations of all these countries enjoy high standards of living and generous welfare systems that ensure most people have a comfortable life.

Map labels: RUSSIA · FINLAND · L A P L A N D · Arctic Circle · North Cape · Tromso · Haltiatunturi 1324m · Kebnekaise 2123m · KJØLEN MOUNTAINS · VESTERÅLEN · LOFTEN · NORWEGIAN SEA · Oulu · Oulujärvi · Inarijärvi · Kemi · Tana · Torne · Lule · Skellefteälv · Umeälv · Umeå · othnia

Scale: Miles 0 50 100 150 200 · Kilometres 0 50 100 150 200 250 300

Globe map labels: ARCTIC OCEAN · BARENTS SEA · RUSSIA · FINLAND · NORWEGIAN SEA · SWEDEN · NORWAY · DENMARK · Skagerrak · Gulf of Bothnia · BALTIC SEA · ESTONIA · LATVIA · LITHUANIA · RUSSIA · POLAND · GERMANY · CZECH REP. · SWITZERLAND · LUXEMBOURG · BELGIUM · NETHERLANDS · ENGLAND · WALES · SCOTLAND · IRELAND · NORTH SEA · ATLANTIC OCEAN · Bay of Biscay · FRANCE · SPAIN

Volvo
Sweden's economy relies heavily on just a few big companies including Volvo. Typical of the Swedish approach, workers in Volvo's car factory build cars in teams so they get the satisfaction of building a complete car.

Little bricks
Denmark is the home of Lego, which was created here in the 1930s. In fact, the word 'Lego' comes from two Danish words *leg* and *godt*, meaning 'play well'. There is now a massive theme park called Legoland made entirely from Lego, 5 km from Copenhagen.

Scandinavian dish
Fish and bread play a big part in Scandinavian food. One of the specialities is the smörgasbord. Smörgas is Swedish for bread and bord means table. But it is much more than the name suggests: it is a delicious spread of cold foods, especially fish such as herring and salmon; also cheeses.

Cool days
Children in Norway have to get used to the cold winters. Even in winter, infants are wrapped in sheepskins and put outside to nap. And when it comes to going to school, which many Norwegian children start as young as two years old, they strap on skis or sometimes skates and head off through the snow.

Wooden church
Some of Norway's wooden churches, called stave churches, date back 900 years to shortly after the time Vikings were converted to Christianity. There are now only 29 left. They are masterpieces of woodwork, built entirely without nails using an ingenious system of curved wooden posts called staves.

Clean living
The Swedish are very conscious of the environment. Recycling schemes are widespread, while to conserve energy, Stockholm's power stations pump excess hot water into the city's homes to provide heating.

and Sweden were the land of the Vikings. These fierce, bold people ventured far from home in their remarkable longships. Viking raids caused terror in Britain and France. The Vikings were masterful seamen and their voyages took them not only to Iceland and Greenland but right across the Atlantic to Newfoundland.

The Scandinavians

The Scandinavians are known for their blonde hair, fair skins – and modern, enlightened way of life. They pay high taxes, but benefits are generous, and more women can work and reach the top than anywhere else in the world. But the divorce rate is high, and only just over half of Scandinavian children are brought up by married parents.

Clean design
Scandinavian homes are admired for their clean and stylish design.

Working up a sweat
Nearly every home in Finland has a sauna – a small, wood-lined room heated to a high temperature with a dry heat, where people go to relax. They are often built near lakes so you can finish off with a cold dip in summer – or in winter a naked roll in the snow.

Vikings
A thousand years ago, Norway

The Little Mermaid
By the shore in Denmark's capital, Copenhagen, sits a statue of the little mermaid, a character created by Danish author Hans Christian Andersen (1805–75). Son of a poor shoemaker, his world-famous fairy tales include 'The Tin Soldier', 'The Snow Queen' and 'The Ugly Duckling'.

Danish bacon
Danish farms are famous for their butter and bacon – and their effective marketing.

Deep fjord
Norway's long and rugged coastline is dominated by fjords. These inlets were gouged out by glaciers in the Ice Ages and are incredibly deep, allowing big ships to sail far inland between high mountains.

Ski country
Norwegians have known for thousands of years that the best way to get around on snow is on skis. Wooden skis covered in animal furs dating back 2300 years were found recently. The word 'ski' is Norwegian and the modern sport of skiing has its roots here in Telemark country. Cross-country skiing is very popular.

NORWAY

SWEDEN

FINLAND

Lahti
Tampere
HELSINKI
Espoo
Vantaa
Pori
Turku
ÅLAND (to Finland)

Gulf of Finland

Glittertind 2472m
Bergen
OSLO
Drammen
Stavanger
Kristiansand

Ljusnan
Dal
Uppsala
STOCKHOLM
Västerås
Örebro
Linköping
Jönköping
Visby
GOTLAND (to Sweden)
ÖLAND

Klar
Vättern
Vänern
Göta
Lägen
Mjøsa
Glåma

BALTIC SEA

Gulf of Bothnia

Kattegat

Göteborg
Helsingborg
COPENHAGEN
Malmö
BORNHOLM (to Denmark)

Ålborg
Randers
Århus
Odense
Kolding
Esbjerg

DENMARK

GERMANY

NORTH SEA

Skagerrak

Did you know? Stockholm is built on 14 islands in the middle of an archipelago of more than 24,000 islands.

Did you know? Norway's people have twice rejected membership of the European Union.

43

Italy

A narrow, often mountainous country, washed almost right round by the Mediterranean Sea, Italy is steeped in history. It is a country of contrasts – the cool, moist north with its prosperous industrial cities; the rich farmland and great 'art' cities (such as Florence) of Tuscany and Umbria; and the hot, dusty south with its poor fields and half-deserted villages.

FACE THE FACTS...

❖ The land
Italy's highest mountain is Monte Rosa at 4638 m – actually it is a mountain massif, with several high points. The longest river is the Po, flowing across the north Italian plain into the Adriatic south of Venice (652 km).

❖ Climate
Italy's climate is typically Mediterranean with hot summers and mild winters, though in the north winters can get quite cool.

❖ Population
57.6 m, a third of whom live in the Po Valley.

❖ Capital
The capital is Rome, once the centre of the Roman Empire.

❖ Resources
Italy has few mineral resources, except for natural gas and marble.

❖ Farming
There are vines and olives almost everywhere for Italy is the world's largest producer of both wine

and olive oil. The richest farmland is in the north in the Po valley, where rows of apple and pear trees grow between strips of wheat and maize and there are acres of sugar beet, artichokes, and tomatoes. Oranges, grapes and olives grow in the dry south. Pigs and beef cattle are widely reared.

❖ Fishing
Italy has a huge fishing fleet, but catches have been reduced by the twin problems of shrinking fish stocks and pollution.

❖ Industry
Italy is one of the world's largest industrial nations – but almost all the industry is in the north of the country, where they make cars, computers, chemicals, textiles, processed food and fashion items.

❖ Government
Italy is a republic with an elected president and two houses of parliament (the Chamber of Deputies and the Senate). Italian politics are volatile with fierce disputes and governments

frequently brought down by scandal. Some politicians want to set up a separate parliament in the north.

❖ Currency
The Italian currency is the Euro.

❖ Religion
Ninety-five per cent of Italians are Roman Catholic Christians. The Pope, the head of the Roman Catholic Church, lives in the Vatican in Rome, headquarters of the Roman Catholic faith worldwide.

❖ Sport
Italians are mad keen on football and motor racing. Card games are also very popular.

Italian cars
Car-making is at the heart of the north's industrial success. Ferrari sports cars are made here, but the giant among car manufacturers is Fiat, based at Turin. For a long time, half the cars in Italy were Fiats, and it was Fiat that introduced the idea of the 'baby' car or mini to the world.

The leaning tower
The towns of northern and central Italy are full of beautiful historic buildings. One of the most photographed is the bell tower of Pisa cathedral – built on soft ground in 1174, it leans over a

Chianti country
The famous wine Chianti is made from grapes grown in Tuscany in the centre of Italy. This is an attractive region of rolling hills covered with vineyards, olive groves and wheatfields and dotted with ancient farms and villages perched on hilltops. Very few Italians live here now, and many of the old villas have been bought by northern Europeans as holiday homes.

Venice
The surprising, beautiful city of Venice is set on 117 islands in a lagoon. Instead of roads, there are 177 canals. Instead of cars there are boats, including the famous gondola, propelled with one oar. Engineers are working to save the city from sinking into the lagoon.

The Vatican
Rome's Vatican City is the world's smallest independent state. Centred on the vast domed cathedral of St Peter's, it is the seat of the Roman Catholic church.

Right, one of the Vatican's Swiss guards, who wear medieval uniform.

Poor south
Olives grow well in the warm, dry climate of the south of Italy, but the *Mezzogiorno* has few other economic strengths – except for organized crime, which has a stranglehold here. Huge amounts of money put in by the state to boost industry mysteriously 'disappear', leaving millions unemployed.

the north, rice and polenta are often preferred to pasta.

houses. The most famous is Milan's La Scala. Italian tenor Luciano Pavarotti is an international star.

Pasta, Parma ham and Parmesan
Italian specialities include Parmesan cheese and Parma ham from the Parma region and pasta – supposedly brought back from China by Marco Polo in the 13th century.

Tourist heaven
The Italian coast is a magnet for tourists – especially the island of Capri. Just a short hydrofoil ride from Naples, the island is often besieged by daytrippers.

1948 Ferrari

O Sole Mio
The Italians have three great passions – fast cars, football and opera. Italy is the home of opera. It was invented here in the 16th century, and some of the greatest of all operas were written by Italians – Verdi's La Traviata, Puccini's La Bohème and Rossini's Barber of Seville. Italians of all classes love opera, and there is an opera house in most cities, invariably playing to packed, enthusiastic

Lunchtime
Mealtimes are important family occasions in Italy, and on warm days a common sight is all the family at lunch round a big table shaded by vines. A typical meal involves antipasto (often cold meats), followed by pasta, then meat or fish with vegetables and salad. But food varies from region to region. In

Sistine chapel ceiling
Many Italian cities and villages are treasure-houses of art. The great artists of the Renaissance – such masters as Leonardo da Vinci, Michelangelo and Raphael – left them with an incomparable array of works. Nowadays, thousands of people crowd into the Sistine Chapel in Rome every month in order to see the great masterpiece by Michelangelo that adorns the ceiling.

Roman circus
Rome has been one of the world's great cities for longer than 2000 years. It is a modern, bustling capital, but the traffic dodges around spectacular ruins dating back to the time of the Roman Empire. Most spectacular of all the ruins is the Colosseum, the Ancient Romans' vast sports arena, which could hold 55,000 spectators.

The lost city
The Ancient Roman town of Pompeii is one of the world's greatest archaeological sites. When the volcano Mt. Vesuvius erupted in AD 79, Pompeii was buried under volcanic ash. It was rediscovered 17 centuries later, almost perfectly preserved under the ash.

Live volcano
Tiny Stromboli is one of the Lipari Islands off southwest Italy and one of the country's two active volcanoes. The other is Mt. Etna, on Sicily. Stromboli continually spews out showers of hot cinders.

The brotherhood
Sicily is the home of the notorious Mafia, whose tentacles extend worldwide. Mafiosi first appeared in the 1800s as groups of Sicilian brigands who made their own justice. Now they are basically gangsters who make money from drug trafficking and corruption on government contracts. Despite repeated police efforts to crack down on them, the Mafia still have a powerful hold in the region.

Italians

The Italians are relaxed, passionate people with a strong sense of family. Although Italian families are smaller than they used to be, a higher proportion of Italians still get married than any other Europeans – and fewer get divorced. But there are wide differences across the country. Italy did not become a single nation until 1861, and even today many think of themselves as, for example, Venetians or Romans first, and as Italians second.

Dressing with style
Italians in the north at least are very concerned about their bella figura – their image – and most dress well. The fashion trade is now big business in Italy, and Italian fashion labels such as Armani, Versace, Valentino, Moschino and Gucci are now world famous. The big fashion city is Milan, although there are also many designer stores in Florence and Rome. The look is generally simple, elegant, high quality – and expensive.

CORSICA (to France)

SARDINIA

I.Asinara

Tirso

Cagliari ○

I.di S. Pietro

SEA

ROME ○
VATICAN CITY

Volturno

Naples ○
ISCHIA
Vesuvius △1277m
Salerno
CAPRI

○ Foggia

○ Bari

○ Taranto
Gulf of Taranto

IONIAN SEA

○ Reggio di Calabria

LIPARI ISLANDS

Messina ○
Mt. Etna 3323m ▲
SICILY
○ Catania

● Palermo

EGADI ISLANDS

Sicilian Channel

PANTELLERIA

Malta Channel
MALTA
VALLETTA ■

MEDITERRANEAN SEA

Miles
0 25 50 75 100

Kilometres
0 50 100 150

Spain and Portugal

Spain and Portugal are cut off from the rest of Europe by the Pyrenees mountains on a peninsula called Iberia. In the north and west is the moist, cool Atlantic coast. In the south is the warm Mediterranean coast. In between is the vast, dry plateau of the Meseta. Here farmers make their living much as they have done for centuries, but elsewhere Spanish cities such as Barcelona have become among the most dynamic and modern in Europe.

Swordfish
Much of Portugal is comparatively undeveloped. Most people still live in the country growing wheat, rice, almonds, olives and maize. Fish play an important part in Portuguese food, and swordfish stew called *bacalão* is a speciality.

Steel city
Situated at the heart of a large industrial and coal-mining area, Bilbao is one of Spain's largest and oldest industrial cities. Like Toledo in the south, it was once famous for the fine steel it made for swords.

FACE THE FACTS...

Mediterranean climate.

❖ **The land**
The highest mountain in mainland Spain is Mulhacén (3477 m); the longest river is the Tagus (1007 km). The Canary Islands, some 1000 km southwest of the south coast, are Spain's.

❖ **Climate**
The centre has cold winters and very hot summers, while the north and west are moist, with cool winters and warm summers. The south coast has a typical

and dusty for some crops, but the warmth is good for olives, sunflowers, grapes, oranges and lemons, as well as for tomatoes, cucumbers, rice and cereals. Goats and sheep are reared in drier areas, cows in the north.

❖ **Forestry**
Nearly a third of Portugal is covered in forests of pine, cork oak, eucalyptus and chestnut. Cork oaks are widespread.

❖ **Fishing**
Fishing is one of the main

❖ **Population**
Spain has a population of 39.4 m; Portugal's is 9.9 m.

❖ **Capitals**
Spain, Madrid; Portugal, Lisbon.

❖ **Natural resources**
Mineral resources are few but valued. They include coal, iron-ore, oil, wolfram and copper.

❖ **Farming**
Parts of the centre are too hot

industries in Portugal and the northwest of Spain, and boats venture far into the Atlantic to catch tuna, sardines, swordfish and anchovies.

❖ **Industry and commerce**
Spain is one of Europe's largest car-makers with major factories in Valencia and Saragossa. It also makes a great deal of steel (in the north), textiles, chemicals (around Bilbao, Madrid and Saragossa), and consumer goods such as refrigerators, washing machines and TVs. Tourism is

also a major industry in this region.

❖ **Government**
Portugal is a republic with an elected president; Spain has a monarch but is governed by an elected parliament called the Cortes headed by a prime minister. Each of 17 Spanish regions also has its own local parliament.

❖ **Languages**
The main language of Spain is Spanish or Castilian, but there are various other languages including Catalan and Basque. In Portugal, they speak Portuguese.

❖ **Currency**
In both Spain and Portugal, the Euro became the sole official currency on 1 January 2002.

❖ **Sport**
The main sport is football.

❖ **Religion**
The vast majority are Roman Catholic.

Design city
Barcelona is the largest seaport and industrial city in Spain, and capital of Catalonia, a region of Spain with its own language. One of Spain's most glamorous cities, where the modern mixes with the traditional.

Miles
0
50
100
150

Kilometres
0
50
100
150
200

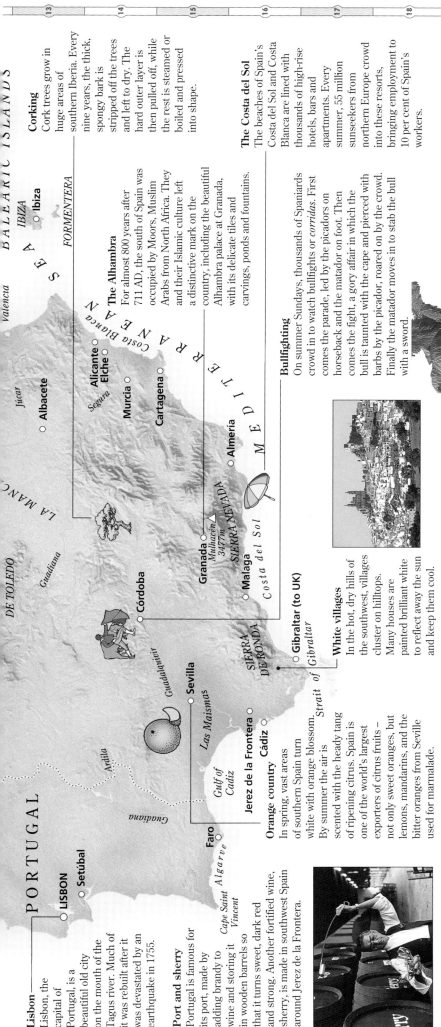

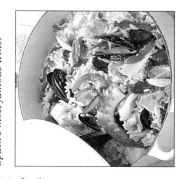

Lisbon
Lisbon, the capital of Portugal, is a beautiful old city on the mouth of the Tagus river. Much of it was rebuilt after it was devastated by an earthquake in 1755.

Port and sherry
Portugal is famous for its port, made by adding brandy to wine and storing it in wooden barrels so that it turns sweet, dark red and strong. Another fortified wine, sherry, is made in southwest Spain around Jerez de la Frontera.

Corking
Cork trees grow in huge areas of southern Iberia. Every nine years, the thick, spongy bark is stripped off the trees and left to dry. The hard outer layer is then pulled off, while the rest is steamed or boiled and pressed into shape.

The Costa del Sol
The beaches of Spain's Costa del Sol and Costa Blanca are lined with thousands of high-rise hotels, bars and apartments. Every summer, 55 million sunseekers from northern Europe crowd into these resorts, bringing employment to 10 per cent of Spain's workers.

The Alhambra
For almost 800 years after 711 AD, the south of Spain was occupied by Moors, Muslim Arabs from North Africa. They and their Islamic culture left a distinctive mark on the country, including the beautiful Alhambra palace at Granada, with its delicate tiles and carvings, ponds and fountains.

Bullfighting
On summer Sundays, thousands of Spaniards crowd in to watch bullfights or *corridas*. First comes the parade, led by the picadors on horseback and the matador on foot. Then comes the fight, a gory affair in which the bull is taunted with the cape and pierced with barbs by the picador, roared on by the crowd. Finally the matador moves in to stab the bull with a sword.

Orange country
In spring, vast areas of southern Spain turn white with orange blossom. By summer the air is scented with the heady tang of ripening citrus. Spain is one of the world's largest exporters of citrus fruits – not only sweet oranges, but lemons, mandarins, and the bitter oranges from Seville used for marmalade.

White villages
In the hot, dry hills of the southwest, villages cluster on hilltops. Many houses are painted brilliant white to reflect away the sun and keep them cool.

Spanish dishes
One of the best-known Spanish dishes is paella, which comes originally from Valencia. Made from saffron-flavoured rice mixed with seafood, meat, peppers and olives, it is traditionally cooked in an iron pan over an open fire, and accompanied by Rioja, Spain's most famous wine.

Festival time
Many cities in the south of Spain have annual festivals – religious occasions which people take very seriously. The best known is in Seville. Every day here in the Semana Santa (Holy Week) before Easter, there is a big procession through the streets, with floats carrying icons, crucifixes and so on. Candlelit processions often continue well into the night.

The Spanish
The Spanish are a passionate, talkative people, and they are not all the pious, deeply conservative people they were once thought to be. There have always been strong regional differences, but since the dictator Franco died in 1975 and democracy was restored, young people have been moving to the cities and adopting a far more liberal outlook on life than their parents had.

Fire dance
The flamenco – from Andalucia in southern Spain – is a fiery dance between a man and a woman. Sometimes there is a wailing, passionate song to accompany them. Sometimes there is nothing more than the intense rhythm of the guitar. The man, dressed in tight trousers, stamps and claps his hands, while the woman, wearing a whirling dress, struts and swings her hips and clicks her castanets as the music builds to a climax.

Eating on the move
Dinner can be at 9 pm or later, so many Spaniards love to spend the early evening in tapas bars. Here they can meet people, chat and drink wine while eating little snacks or 'tapas', including olives, slices of tortilla (omelette), patatas bravas (spicy potatoes) and albondigas (meatballs).

Language barrier
The language we know as Spanish comes only from the central region known as Castile. Castilian is the official language and is taught in every school, but Spain has many different languages and cultures, including Catalan and Gallego – and Euskura from the Basque region in northern Spain around San Sebastian.

Some Basques want to be separate from Spain altogether, and the Basque separatist group ETA has been running a terrorist campaign since 1959. Recent years have seen millions of Spaniards marching in the streets to protest against ETA outrages.

Spanish school
Schoolchildren in Spain start early, at around 8 am, but have a long lunch – la comida – often followed by a nap. After school, they have a snack (la merienda) and then go out to play until the family supper at 9 pm.

PORTUGAL
- LISBON
- Setúbal
- Faro
- Algarve
- Cape Saint Vincent
- Jerez de la Frontera
- Cádiz
- Gulf of Cadiz
- Las Maismas
- Sevilla
- Córdoba
- SIERRA DE RONDA
- Gibraltar (to UK)
- Strait of Gibraltar
- Granada
- Mulhacén 3477m
- SIERRA NEVADA
- Málaga
- Costa del Sol
- Almería
- Cartagena
- Murcia
- Albacete
- Alicante
- Elche
- Costa Blanca
- Valencia
- MEDITERRANEAN SEA
- BALEARIC ISLANDS
- IBIZA
- Ibiza
- FORMENTERA
- LA MANCHA
- DE TOLEDO
- Guadiana
- Guadalquivir
- Ardila
- Júcar
- Segura

Did you know? The Basque ball game *pelota vasca* is the fastest ball game in the world.

47

Did you know? In the Altamira cave in northern Spain are paintings dating back 15,000 years.

Did you know? Vlad the Impaler, a 15th-century Eastern European prince, used to impale his many victims on wooden stakes.

Did you know? Poland grows more potatoes than any country but Russia.

Did you know? Romania means 'land of the Romans' – its people descend from Roman settlers.

FACE THE FACTS...

❖ The land
The highest mountains in Eastern Europe are Musala in Bulgaria (2925 m), Mt Olympus in Greece (2917 m) and Mt Triglav in Slovenia (2863 m). The longest rivers are the Danube (2850 km) and the Vistula (1091 km).

❖ Climate
Most of Eastern Europe has a typical temperate climate with cool winters and warm summers. Mountains are snow-covered in winter. Greece, though, is Mediterranean, with hot summers and mild winters.

❖ Population
Poland 38.6 m; Romania 22.4 m; Serbia & Montenegro 10.6 m; Czech Republic 10.2 m; Hungary 10 m; Greece 10.5; Bulgaria 8.2 m; Slovakia 5.4 m; Croatia 4.4 m; Bosnia & Herzegovina 3.9 m; Albania 3.3 m; Macedonia 2 m; Slovenia 2 m.

❖ Capitals
See the map.

❖ Natural resources
Poland has enough coal to meet two-thirds of its energy needs. It also has copper, sulphur and silver deposits. Romania has natural gas. Greece exports a great deal of marble. Hungary and Greece have bauxite (aluminium).

❖ Farming
The lowlands of Eastern Europe are fertile, productive farmland, and countries such as Romania grow good crops of vegetables, flax and hemp as well as vines in places. The main crops are cereals, potatoes and sugar beet. Poland is known for its rye, and the Czech Republic for its hops. On the dry hills of Greece, goats are common. Under communism, many farms in Eastern Europe were run by collectives. Now most farms are private – but production has dropped considerably. In some places, farming methods have changed little in centuries, and horse-drawn ploughs are still a common sight.

❖ Industry and commerce
The years of communism forced the development of heavy metal-based industries in many Eastern European countries. Yugoslavia has extensive engineering industries, while Poland has big steel, ship, vehicle and engineering industries. The Czech Republic is a noted producer of beer.

❖ Government
Until 1989–1990, all of Eastern Europe except for Greece was made up of communist states under the domination of the Soviet Union. Since then, each country has become a democracy with a president.

❖ Religion
Most people in Eastern Europe are Christian, except in Bosnia, Yugoslavia and Albania, where many are Muslim. During the wars in Bosnia, many Muslims were victimized.

❖ Sport
The most popular sport is football.

Eastern Europe

Except for Poland with its wide plains, bogs and lakes, Eastern Europe is very mountainous. The mountains make getting around difficult, but may have helped the identity of individual nations in this region to survive 40 years of Soviet rule, which ended in 1990.

BALTIC SEA
RUSSIA
BELARUS
GERMANY
POLAND
CZECH REPUBLIC
SLOVAKIA
AUSTRIA
UKRAINE
MOLDOVA
HUNGARY
ROMANIA
Gdynia
Gdansk
Szczecin
Bydgoszcz
Poznan
Bialystok
WARSAW
Lodz
Wroclaw
Lublin
Czestochowa
Katowice
Krakow
PRAGUE
Ostrava
Brno
Gerlachovka 2655m
CARPATHIAN MOUNTAINS
Kosice
BRATISLAVA
BUDAPEST
Debrecen
Cluj-Napoca
Iasi
CHISINAU
Vistula
Bug
Oder
Elbe
Danube
Prut
Dniester
CARPATHIAN
Miles 0 50 100 150 200
Kilometres 0 100 200 300

FINLAND
NORWAY
SWEDEN
NORTH SEA
SCOTLAND
ESTONIA
LATVIA
DENMARK
IRELAND
ENGLAND
LITHUANIA
WALES
NETHERLANDS
BELARUS
BELGIUM
GERMANY
POLAND
CZECH REP.
UKRAINE
RUSSIA
FRANCE
SLOVAKIA
MOLDOVA
AUSTRIA
SLOVENIA
HUNGARY
CROATIA
ROMANIA
BOSNIA & HERZEGOVINA
BLACK SEA
GEORGIA
YUGOSLAVIA
BULGARIA
ITALY
MACEDONIA
ALBANIA
TURKEY
GREECE
MEDITERRANEAN SEA
SYRIA
EGYPT

Polish ships
The great shipyards of Gdansk on the Baltic Sea make Poland the world's fifth-largest builder of merchant ships. In 1980, shipyard workers protesting against poor working conditions, led by Lech Walesa, forced the government to recognize Solidarnosc, the first trade union ever legalized in a communist country. It was one of the first steps towards the end of communist domination in Eastern Europe.

The Blue Danube
Despite the name of the famous waltz by Johann Strauss, the River Danube is very rarely blue. No other river in the world is connected to so many countries or flows through three capital cities – Vienna, Budapest and Belgrade. Its rapid current and shallow bed make it hard to navigate.

Sunflower success
The giant sunflower was introduced to Europe from North America in the 1500s. Hungary is now one of the world's leading producers of sunflower oil, and in the summer vast areas of Hungary's Great Plain turn yellow with the huge 30-cm blooms.

Country living
The traditional Romanian cottage is a wooden cabin with a veranda, decorated with beautiful carving, colourful crockery, wall rugs and handmade furniture. But life in the Romanian countryside is far from idyllic – the inhabitants of this area are amongst the poorest in Europe.

A bed of roses

Near the Bulgarian town of Kazanluk, is a valley that every May and June turns a gorgeous pink with the blooms of millions of damask roses – the famous Valley of Roses. Roses are grown here for their essential oil, called attar, which is worth its weight in gold. Petals are picked at dawn before the sun can dry out the oils, and hand-packed into sacks. Some 2000 petals go to make a single gram of attar.

Smoked out

Bulgaria is the world's second-largest exporter of cigarettes. Tobacco grown on the Thracian plain earns more money than any other crop.

Island service

Greece is a country of islands – important island groups include the Cyclades, the Ionians and the Dodecanese. Ships continually ply between the islands and the mainland ports of Athens and Corinth. Most larger islands get at least two ships a day.

Goulash

Hungarians grow two kinds of chilli, and dry and grind them into paprika, used to flavour their speciality – a spicy meat stew called goulash.

Below, kebab, a Greek (and Turkish) speciality.

Greek salad

Goats and olives are at the heart of the Greek diet. Greek salad is a mixture of salad vegetables and olives, along with feta cheese made from goats or sheep's milk. In some small villages, the local baker may allow villagers to bring their own food to cook in his large outdoor oven, or *fuorno*, which holds its heat throughout the day.

Romanian troubles

Romania has not done as well since the collapse of communism as other countries. Many people are poor, because there has been a huge drop in output on the newly private farms. Much the same ruling elite is still in power and as right-wing, nationalistic elements gain influence, the minority Hungarians and Gypsies (or Romanies) suffer from prejudice.

The music tradition

Eastern Europe has a rich heritage of traditional music, including the massed women's choirs of Bulgaria, the gypsy violinists of Romania and the balalaika bands of Macedonia.

Traditional dress at a Polish religious festival.

Broken bridge

The 16th-century bridge at Mostar was one of the casualties of the terrible war that raged through Bosnia and Croatia in the early 1990s. But the real cost was human. Tens of thousands of people were killed. There is so much bitterness that some people doubt if the United Nations soldiers brought in to keep the peace will ever be able to leave.

The Parthenon

In the fifth century BC, Greece, and Athens in particular, was the home to an astonishing flowering of culture that has left its mark on the world. The political and scientific ideas of Ancient Greek thinkers such as Aristotle, the plays of Sophocles, the poems of Homer, the mathematics of Euclid – all have had a huge influence on the Western world. But perhaps the most obvious legacy is the elegant style of Greek architecture – typified by the great temple of the Parthenon, built high on a hill overlooking Athens between 447 and 432 BC.

Going to Greece

The sparkling blue seas around Greece's islands make it one of the world's most popular holiday destinations. More than 10 million visitors come here every year – some to see the relics of Ancient Greece, but most simply to soak up the sun.

The Eastern Europeans

The lives of many Eastern Europeans have changed dramatically since the collapse of communism in 1990. Some cities, such as Prague, Bratislava and Warsaw, are buzzing with wealth and new-found freedoms. Others are facing new poverty as jobs become hard to find and old structures break down. The war-torn countries of the former Yugoslavia are going through a painful period of reconstruction.

Popular Prague

Since it was opened to tourists in 1989, people have flocked to Prague in their millions to wander through its historic streets, ride on its old trams and eat and drink at the hundreds of new restaurants and bars. It has become particularly popular with the media, and many recording artists have worked in studios here.

Divided city

The Bosnian capital of Sarajevo is gradually being rebuilt after the terrible conflict of the early 1990s that saw almost half of Bosnia's 4.5 m people flee the country and more than 140,000 killed or missing. During the war, the city was under constant gunfire from surrounding hills, food was desperately short and many children were badly injured or separated from their families. It will be a long time before the city and its people recover fully from this period.

The Magyars

The Hungarians are descended from the Magyars, a fierce tribe of horsemen who migrated here from the steppes in the east 1000 years ago.

Map labels

BLACK SEA

TURKEY

Constanta

Varna

BUCHAREST

Craiova

Plovdiv

SOFIA

BULGARIA

BALKAN MOUNTAINS

Musala 2925m

Maritsa

Danube

TRANSYLVANIAN ALPS

Danube

Galati

NS

Novi Sad

Sava

Drava

Danube

ZAGREB

Banja Luka

CROATIA

BOSNIA & HERZEGOVINA

SARAJEVO

BELGRADE

YUGOSLAVIA

Nis

SKOPJE

MACEDONIA

Bitola

TIRANA

ALBANIA

Durres

Split

ADRIATIC SEA

Thessaloniki

LIMNOS

LESBOS

KHIOS

AEGEAN SEA

PINDUS MTS

Mount Olympus 2917m

Larissa

GREECE

Patras

ATHENS

CYCLADES

DODECANESE

RHODES

CRETE

Iraklion

MEDITERRANEAN SEA

IONIAN ISLANDS

IONIAN SEA

Asia

Asia is the world's largest continent by some way, and contains two of the world's biggest countries, Russia and China. Dividing it in two are the soaring Himalayas and the high Tibetan plateau.

In 1917, Russia overthrew its emperor to form the Soviet Union, the world's first communist state. In 1911, China forced its last emperor from the throne. By 1949, it too was communist. In the 1950s, North Korea and North Vietnam turned communist too – provoking unsuccessful wars against them by the Americans. In the 1980s, it was possible to travel all the way from Czechoslovakia to China entirely in communist countries. With the disintegration of the Soviet Union in 1990, communism came to an end here, however, and even China has begun to open up a little to the West.

To the south is tropical Asia. Here, most of the rain tends to come in a short rainy season called the monsoon. When it does come it is torrential, watering the small areas of lush tropical jungles that remain in this region.

ARCTIC OC

Barents Sea

● Murmansk

Kara Sea

● St Petersburg

Arctic Circle

BELARUS

Dnieper MOSCOW ○ *Volga*

○ Kiev

UKRAINE

Volga

WESTERN SIBERIAN LOWLAND

R U S

Ob

Yenisey

Istanbul ○ *Black Sea*

Volgograd ○

Ural ● Omsk

● Novosibirsk

Irtysh

Ishim

ANKARA ○

TURKEY

GEORGIA

CAUCASUS MTS.

Mediterranean Sea

ARMENIA

Caspian Sea

KAZAKHSTAN

Aral Sea

UZBEKISTAN *Syr Dar'ya*

Lake Balkhash

SAYAN M

ALTAI MOUNT

LEBANON

ISRAEL SYRIA

JORDAN

AZERBAIJAN

Euphrates *Tigris*

Amu Dar'ya

TURKMENISTAN

BISHKEK ○

TIEN SHAN

BAGHDAD ○

ASHKHABAD ○

TASHKENT ○ KYRGYZSTAN

TAJIKISTAN

Taklimakan Desert

KUNLAN SH

IRAQ

TEHRAN ●

ZAGROS MTS.

I R A N

DUSHANBE ○

AFGHANISTAN

KABUL ○

KARAKORAM RANGE

KUWAIT

HINDU KUSH

Red Sea

SAUDI

RIYADH ○

ISLAMABAD ○

○ Lahore

PLATEAU OF TIBET

QATAR

ARABIA UNITED ARAB EMIRATES

PAKISTAN

Indus

H I M A L A Y A S

ARABIAN PENINSULA

Karachi ○

NEW ○ NEPAL ○

DELHI *Mt. Everest* △ BHUTAN

Ganges

SANA'A ● OMAN

YEMEN

Arabian Sea

I N D I A

BANGLADE

Gulf of Aden

Calcutta ○ DHAK

Mumbai ○ *Deccan*

Bay of Bengal (M

Hyderabad ○

RANGOO

Madras ○

I N D I A N

COLOMBO ○ SRI LANKA

O C E A N

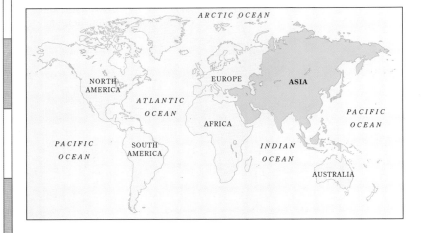

ARCTIC OCEAN

NORTH AMERICA

EUROPE ASIA

ATLANTIC OCEAN

AFRICA

PACIFIC OCEAN

PACIFIC OCEAN

SOUTH AMERICA

INDIAN OCEAN

AUSTRALIA

Miles 0   200   400   600   800   1000

Kilometres 0   400   800   1200   1500

To the north is the huge expanse of Siberia and Mongolia, with grassy plains stretching as far as the eye can see. Beyond them are vast coniferous forests, and further north still, the empty Arctic tundra. Asia is a land of extremes. The very centre is thousands of kilometres from the sea, resulting in a climate where winters are icy cold and summers are baking hot. In Yakutsk in Siberia, winter temperatures can plunge below −64°C and summer temperatures can climb to 39°C.

Two out of every three people in the world live in Asia. China and India alone are home to 40 per cent of the world's population. Asia has been farmed for longer than anywhere in the world. Farming was flourishing along the banks of the Tigris and Euphrates in the Middle East more than 7000 years ago, and it began in China along the banks of the Yellow River about the same time. Along with farming developed the world's oldest civilizations. The first Chinese cities date back to the time of the Longshan people, 4500 years ago. The first cities in the Middle East were built at least 7000 years ago.

Out to the east of Asia is Japan. Japan was defeated in World War II, and two of its major cities, Hiroshima and Nagasaki, were destroyed by American atomic bombs. However, thanks to hard work and innovation, Japan has become the world's largest economy, competing with the USA's in the 1990s. Then in 1998 Japan was overtaken by a severe financial crisis caused largely by unwise lending and borrowing. The future remains uncertain.

A few southeast Asian countries, such as South Korea, Singapore and Malaysia, did so well economically in the 1980s that people began to talk of them as the 'tiger economies'. Heavy foreign investment and cheap, skilled labour helped these countries become the fastest growing economies in the world, with astonishingly successful electronics, car-making and shipbuilding industries. Then in the late 1990s their fortunes declined dramatically. As with Japan, their outlook remains uncertain.

FACE THE FACTS...

❖ **The land**
The highest peak is Mt Garmo in Tajikistan (7495 m). Some of the world's longest rivers flow here: the Ob'-Irtysh (5570 km), the Lena (4393 km), and the Volga (3690 km).

❖ **Climate**
A huge range, from the tundra of the Arctic north to the southern deserts.

❖ **Population**
Russia 146.2 m; Ukraine 49.9 m;
Uzbekistan 24.4 m; Kazakhstan 14.9 m; Azerbaijan 8 m; Georgia 5.4 m; Tajikistan 6.2 m; Kyrgyzstan 4.8 m; Turkmenistan 4.7 m; Armenia 3.8 m.

❖ **Capitals**
See the map.

❖ **Natural resources**
Russia and its neighbours have some of the richest mineral deposits in the world. Azerbaijan and western Siberia have huge deposits of oil and natural gas; there is also coal, iron ore, copper, gold, nickel, and much more.

❖ **Farming**
Barely 10 per cent of Russia is farmed, but this is a huge area and makes it one of the world's main growers of barley, oats, rye, wheat and potatoes.

❖ **Industry and commerce**
The Soviet Union invested heavily in industry.

❖ **Government**
The Communist Party held power in the Soviet Union (the USSR) until 1991, when the USSR was dissolved.

The 15 republics of the Union then got their own governments.

❖ **Religion**
Most Russians are Russian Orthodox Christians; most southern states are Muslim.

Language
More than 80 languages are spoken; Russian is spoken by 52 per cent.

Sport
Ice hockey, ice skating, football, swimming and gymnastics.

The Kremlin
The Kremlin is the old centre of government in the middle of Moscow. Its origins date back to the wooden fort begun in 1147 by Prince Yuri Dolgoruki. It is now a vast collection of palaces, offices, churches, museums and monuments.

Mother Volga
The River Volga has been central to Russian life for centuries, and the subject of songs and poems. Far from the oceans, Russians relied on this essential link to the sea in a land where there are few good roads. Now many goods go by rail, but the Volga remains an important transport route.

Nuclear disaster
In 1986, a nuclear reactor blew up in the Chernobyl power station north of Kiev in the Ukraine. It was the world's worst nuclear power accident. Radioactivity was released over a wide area – it reached Scandinavia and Britain. Ukraine and Belarus are, geographically, parts of Europe, together with European Russia which extends as far east as the Ural Mountains.

These three countries are actually part of Europe. See also page 33.

Grain baskets
Vast areas of the Ukraine and much of southern Russia are flat plains known as steppes. Here in the fertile black soil, more than a quarter of the world's grain is grown. Russians eat huge amounts of cereals.

The Cosmodrome
The world's first artificial satellite, *Sputnik 1,* was launched in 1957 from the 'Cosmodrome' at Baykonur in the empty heart of Kazakhstan – and so was the first man in space, Yuri Gagarin, in 1961.

Georgia
Georgia is a small, mountainous country perched between Europe and Asia. The capital, Tbilisi, is said to be one of the oldest cities in the world.

Caspian oil
Oil beneath the Caspian Sea off Azerbaijan once enabled the Soviet Union to produce half the world's oil. Now even larger oil and gas reserves have been found here, and in nearby Kazakhstan, Turkmenistan and Uzbekistan too.

The road to Samarkand
Samarkand in Uzbekistan is one of the oldest cities in Asia, lying on the Silk Road, the ancient trading route that linked China to the Middle East and Europe in the Middle Ages.

ARCTIC

FRANZ JOSEF LAND

NORTHE
LAND

Barents Sea

Novaya
Zemlya

Kara Sea

Murmansk

FINLAND

Arkhangel'sk

TALLINN
ESTONIA

LITHUANIA
RUSSIA
LATVIA
RIGA

St Petersburg

VILIUS

MINSK

POLAND

BELARUS

SLOVAKIA

Homyel

HUNGARY

Chernobyl

MOSCOW

Northern Dvina

Volga

ROMANIA

UKRAINE

KIEV

Nizhniy Novgorod

Dniepr

Don

Kharkov

MOLDOVA

Odessa

Voronezh

Dnipropetrovsk

Donetsk

Black Sea

Rostov-na-Donu

Kazan

Simbirsk

Togliatti

Saratov

Samara

Ufa

Volga

Volgograd

Ural

Izhevsk

Perm

Yekaterinburg

Chelyabinsk

URAL MOUNTAINS

WESTERN SIBERIAN LOWLAND

Ob'

Ob'

Yenisey

R U S
S

Omsk

Krasnoya

Novosibirsk

CAUCASUS MTS

Astrakhan

Mount Elbrus 5642m △

Kutaisi

GEORGIA

TBILISI

ARMENIA

YEREVAN

AZERBAIJAN

AZER.

BAKU

TURKEY

Caspian Sea

AKMOLA

Pavlodar

K A Z A K H S T A N

Aral Sea

SAYAN
MOUNTAI

ALTAI
MOUNTAINS

Karaganda

Lake Balkhash

UZBEKISTAN

Syr Dar'ya

Amu Dar'ya

TURKMENISTAN

ASHKHABAD

Samarkand

Chardzhou

IRAN

AFGHANISTAN

PAKISTAN

TASHKENT

BISHKEK

Almaty

KYRGYZSTAN

Osh

Tien Shan

DUSHANBE

△ Garmo 7495m

TAJIKISTAN

Irtysh

Ishim

CHIN

Miles	0	100	200	300	400	500	600	700
Kilometres	0	200	400	600	800	1000		

Turkmenistan carpet.

Northern Asia

Until 1991, the whole of northern Asia and far-eastern Europe were joined in a single gigantic country, the Soviet Union. Now it is split into 15 separate republics. The largest of them, the Russian Federation – or just plain Russia – is still the world's largest country by far. West of the Urals is generally well-populated. To the east and north are the vast empty expanses of Siberia.

Chukchi Sea

Bering Strait

ARCTIC OCEAN

FINLAND
LATVIA
ESTONIA
LITHUANIA
BELARUS
POLAND
UKRAINE
GREECE
TURKMENISTAN
AFGHANISTAN
SAUDI ARABIA
PAKISTAN
INDIA
RUSSIA
KAZAKHSTAN
UZBEKISTAN
MONGOLIA
NORTH KOREA
CHINA
JAPAN
PHILIPPINES
MALAYSIA
INDONESIA
INDIAN OCEAN
AUSTRALIA
NEW ZEALAND
ALASKA
Bering Sea
PACIFIC OCEAN

East Siberian Sea

'Onion domes', characteristic of Russian religious buildings.

Bering Sea

NEW SIBERIAN ISLANDS

Laptev Sea

C E A N

KOLYMA MOUNTAINS

Arctic Circle

The Russian bear
Russia is famous for its fur-bearing animals – whose coats in the past gave essential warm winter clothing. The huge brown bear became a symbol for all Russia, and for kindness and wisdom. It now lives only in Siberia and the Far East.

Lena
VERKHOYANSKI MOUNTAINS

Magadan ○

KAMCHATKA

CENTRAL SIBERIAN PLATEAU

Yakutsk ○

Sea of Okhotsk

Trans-Siberian Railway
The Trans-Siberian Railway is the world's longest railway, stretching more than 9300 km from Moscow's Yaroslavl Station in the west to Vladivostok on the Sea of Japan in the east. The entire journey takes about a week.

I A

Lena

STANOVY MOUNTAINS

Amur

KURIL ISLANDS

SAKHALIN

at nursery school, and gymnastics are compulsory at junior school. At seven, promising gymnasts are selected by their teachers to go to special training schools.

Lake Baikal

YABLONOVY MOUNTAINS

Amur

SIKHOTE-ALIN MOUNTAINS

Sea of Japan

JAPAN

Irkutsk ○

CHINA

Vladivostok ○

Flat-life
Two-thirds of Russians live in cities and there is a real shortage of accommodation. People wanting a flat have to put their name down on a waiting list, and newly married couples usually have to live with their parents. Most flats are very small, with just two main rooms – one serves as a living room and a bedroom for the parents; the children sleep and do their homework in the other room.

sey

M O N G O L I A

The Russians

With the break-up of the Soviet Union, Russians are trying to adapt to change. For most people in the country and small towns, life has changed little. But in cities such as Moscow and St Petersburg, people have become much more money-conscious. For the first time, a few ordinary Russians are becoming very rich – often from the black market. Shops are being stocked with hi-fis, food and other luxuries that were not available before.

Kazakhs
The Soviet Union was dominated by Russians. But there was an astonishing variety of people and cultures within the USSR, many with their own language and traditions – including the Cossacks or Kazakhs, a fiercely independent, nomadic people, skilled with horses and recognizable by their colourful and distinctive costumes. Wealth from oil has brought the Kazakhs a new sense of pride in their culture.

Yakutia
The Yakut people are still within

the Russian Federation. They live in one of the coldest, most remote parts of eastern Siberia, along the Lena river. Yakutia is rich in diamonds and coal, and the Yakuts are now in conflict with the Russians for control of these resources.

Russian steps
Although ballet came originally from France in the 19th century, the Russians made it their own, and the Bolshoi of Moscow and the Kirov of St Petersburg are among the world's most famous ballet companies.

Russian jumps
Young Russian gymnasts are among the best in the world. Children start

Borsch and beef
A traditional Russian lunch begins with zakuski (cold meats and pickled cucumbers, spring onions and caviar). This is followed by soup, then meat (or fish) and potatoes, finishing with sweets and strong coffee. A Russian speciality is borsch, beetroot soup.

Did you know? The name 'Russian' could come from a Viking word meaning oarsmen or sailors.

53

Southwest Asia

Much of Southwest Asia is hot, dry, rocky desert and some of it – like the Rub' al Khali or Empty Quarter of Saudi Arabia – is almost uninhabited. There are mountains, too, where winters can be bitterly cold: these include the Asir mountains of Yemen, the high plateaux of Iran and Turkey and the Hindu Kush of Afghanistan. In between, though, there are fertile plains and valleys. And all around the Gulf are the oil wells that have brought the region its new wealth.

FACE THE FACTS...

❖ Land
The highest points include Nowshak in Afghanistan (7485 m), Damavand in Iran (5671 m), Mt Ararat in Turkey (5123 m). The longest river is the Euphrates in Iraq/Syria (2815 km).

❖ Population
Iran 63 m; Turkey 64.3 m; Afghanistan 25.8 m; Iraq 22.7 m; Saudi Arabia 20.1 m; Syria 15.7 m; Yemen 17 m; Israel 6.1 m;

Jordan 4.7 m; Lebanon 4.2 m; Kuwait 1.9 m; United Arab Emirates 2.8 m; Oman 2.3 m; Bahrain 666,000; Qatar 565,000.

❖ Capitals
See the map.

❖ Natural resources
The gigantic oil reserves of the Middle East dominate the economy of the Gulf states. Saudi Arabia is the world's number one exporter of oil and second producer after Russia. It has 25

per cent of the world's known reserves. Within the Gulf itself, Saudi Arabia has 46.6 per cent of the oil, Iran 19.5 per cent, UAE 13 per cent, Kuwait 10.5 per cent, Oman 4 per cent, Qatar 2.6 per cent, Iraq 2.5 per cent, Yemen and Bahrain 1.3 per cent. Saudi Arabia also has gold, silver and copper. Afghanistan is the oldest and most famous lapis lazuli producer in the world. Turkey has chrome, boron and brown coal.

❖ Farming
It may have been in this part of

the world that people first learned to farm, more than 10,000 years ago. Now, where land can be irrigated, people grow dates, figs and other fruit, lentils, olives, sugar, cotton and cereals. Sheep and goats are raised on high ground. Israel is famous for Jaffa oranges. Oman grows trees for frankincense.

❖ Industry
Only Israel has a significant manufacturing industry that is not oil-based, though a range of industries are developing in

Syria, Turkey and Iran, including carpets, textiles, glassware, cement, metal products, cars, fertilizers, chemicals, plastics, and food products such as sugar.

❖ Government
Many of the Arab countries of the Middle East are dominated by Islamic law, and ruled by kings, emirs, sheikhs and sultans who have absolute power. Turkey, the Lebanon and Yemen are multi-party democratic republics, like Israel. Iraq is controlled by the Revolutionary Command Council.

❖ Religion
Except in Israel, where most people follow the Jewish faith, the vast majority of people in southwest Asia are Muslims. In Lebanon, 25 per cent of people are Christian.

❖ Sport
Horse racing is popular in many Arab countries, especially Saudi Arabia and Iraq, and football is popular almost everywhere.

Istanbul
Standing at the meeting point of Europe and Asia, Istanbul is Turkey's biggest city and main port. Known as both Byzantium and Constantinople in the past, it blends the ancient with the modern and west with east – a bustling crowded city full of hurrying people and hooting taxis. The Hagia Sophia is one of the city's most famous landmarks. It was built as a cathedral in the 5th century then converted to a mosque in the 15th.

Petra
The ancient city of Petra in Jordan is one of the most breathtaking sites in the Middle East – vast, pink sandstone ruins hewn out of the rock by the Nabataeans in the 4th century BC.

Rebuilding Beirut
Beirut, capital of Lebanon, was once a beautiful, lively city with four universities. But civil war in the 1970s and 1980s ravaged the city. Recently, the job of

Did you know? Persian carpets are not just for walking on – people eat, sleep and pray on them.

INDIAN OCEAN

CHINA
NEPAL
INDIA
SRI LANKA
PAKISTAN
AFGHANISTAN
TURKMENISTAN
UZBEKISTAN
KAZAKHSTAN
Aral Sea
RUSSIA
Caspian Sea
IRAN
Arabian Sea
BAHRAIN
QATAR
UNITED ARAB EMIRATES
OMAN
SAUDI ARABIA
YEMEN
IRAQ
SYRIA
TURKEY
JORDAN
ISRAEL
LEBANON
CYPRUS
Red Sea
ERITREA
ETHIOPIA
SUDAN
EGYPT
LIBYA
Mediterranean Sea
ITALY
GREECE
YUGOSLAVIA
BULGARIA
ROMANIA
HUNGARY
AUSTRIA
CZECH REPUBLIC
SLOVAKIA
MOLDOVA
UKRAINE
POLAND
BELARUS
GERMANY
Black Sea
ARMENIA
AZERBAIJAN
GEORGIA

Miles 0 100 200 300 400
Kilometres 0 100 200 300 400 500 600

HINDU KUSH
Nausnak 7483m
KABUL
Herat
Kandahar
AFGHANISTAN
Mashhad
TURKMENISTAN
Dash-e-kavir
CASPIAN SEA
ELBURZ MOUNTAINS
Damavand 5771m
TEHRAN
Qom
Kashan
Esfahan
Yazd
ZAGROS MOUNTAIN
AZERBAIJAN
Tabriz
Lake Urmia
Aras
ARMENIA
Ararat 5165m
Lake Van
Hamadan
Bakhtaran
Kirkuk
Tigris
Mosul
BAGHDAD
I R A Q
Gaziantep
Aleppo
Euphrates
S Y R I A
Homs
DAMASCUS
Az-Zarqa
AMMAN
Irbid
JORDAN
BEIRUT
LEBANON
Tripoli
Haifa
Tel Aviv-Jaffa
JERUSALEM
ISRAEL
Adana
TAURUS MOUNTAINS
Konya
Lake Tuz
T U R K E Y
ANKARA
Kizil Irmak
NICOSIA
CYPRUS
Limassol
Sakarya
Bursa
Istanbul
Izmir
B L A C K   S E A
MEDITERRANEAN SEA

Carpets

Iran is famous for its carpets (often referred to as Persian carpets) with their beautiful, richly coloured patterns of flowers, leaves and other Islamic symbols. Made from thousands of pieces of wool and silk knotted together by hand, they are produced in village workshops across the country. They have been woven here since at least the 5th century BC.

Building Dubai

Part of the United Arab Emirates, Dubai is just one of the Gulf states to which oil has brought huge wealth. The money is being spent on new buildings, airports, roads, factories, schools and hospitals.

Water from the sea

Gulf states such as Qatar have always been desperately short of water, and people relied on wells for drinking water. Now money from oil is paying for another source. All along the coast, huge desalination plants are being built to take the salt out of sea water and to make it usable in people's homes.

Bazaars

In many Arab countries, people shop in bazaars – narrow, winding passageways, crammed with colourful stalls and booths selling foods and spices, copperware and carpets, jewellery and gems. Prices are rarely fixed, so the bazaar is noisy with the sound of people haggling over how much to pay.

Food on a skewer

When wandering through town, Turkish people often buy shish kebabs – chunks of lamb skewered on a stick with onions and green peppers and grilled over a charcoal glow. Meat in Turkey – typically lamb or chicken – is usually highly seasoned and often served with yoghurt and bread.

Veiled women

Women in many of the Muslim countries of the Middle East are expected to hide themselves away in the presence of men. They wear a robe called an aba or chador which covers the entire body and head. Even the face is covered in a veil or burqa, leaving only the eyes visible. In Saudi Arabia, women are not allowed to drive cars.

The promised land

For thousands of years, the Jews were scattered across the world and often faced persecution. But in 1947 they established their own homeland in Israel and more and more Jews come to live here every year. Some retain strictly traditional ways, but many young Israelis mix old ways with a new Western lifestyle.

Map labels

An Nafud

KUWAIT

Persian Gulf

Dammam
BAHRAIN MANAMA
Ad QATAR
Dahna DOHA

Burudayh

Shaqra

RIYADH

Medina

Jiddah
Taif
Mecca

Tropic of Cancer

SAUDI ARABIA

HIJAZ

RED SEA

ASIR

Tihama

ARABIAN PENINSULA

Rub' al Khali

YEMEN

SANA'A
Hodeida
Ta'iz
Aden
Bab el Mandeb
Gulf of Aden

Mukalla

INDIAN OCEAN

Strait of Hormuz
OMAN
Dubai
MUSCAT
Sohar
Gulf of Oman

UNITED ARAB EMIRATES
ABU DHABI

OMAN

ARABIAN SEA

Salalah

Sacred city

Jerusalem is one of the oldest cities in the world, dating back more than 6000 years. It contains important sacred sites for three major religions – Christianity, Islam and Judaism.

Bedouins

In the past, many of the desert-dwelling Arab people known as Bedouins were nomads, moving herds of sheep and goats from pasture to pasture. They lived in tents made from black goat hair. Now less than 1 per cent of Arabs are nomads and most Bedouins live in houses, spending only the hot summer months in tents.

Ship of the desert

No large animal is better equipped to cope with the desert than the camel. It can store enough food and fluids for days in the large hump of fat on its back. It is a very placid animal and desert people have used the Arabian or dromedary camel as transport for thousands of years.

The Southwest Asians

The countries of the Near East, especially Israel, have managed to prosper in spite of the tensions created in the region by the bitter enmity between Israelis and Arabs. Because of the wealth that comes with oil, the people of the United Arab Emirates and Qatar have an exceptionally high income per head. Yet some people in Southwest Asia, especially in Yemen and Iraq, remain desperately poor.

The old game

In many places in the Middle East, men often go to coffee houses to drink coffee, chat, smoke cigarettes and pipes, and to play backgammon and cards. Backgammon is an ancient board game that has kept people happily absorbed in this part of the world for thousands of years.

East and west

Many people from Europe, North America and neighbouring Asian countries have come to this region to work on the new building projects. This foreign presence has helped to Westernize the local people, especially the young, and so too does the regular contact with Western countries through business and through the oil trade organization, OPEC. However, most Arabs are committed Muslims and continue to respect traditional ways. Arab businessmen often attend business meetings in traditional flowing robes.

Did you know? Many Israelis live in rural settlements called *kibbutzim*, with shared facilities.

55

Did you know? Jainist monks respect all life and so wear masks to prevent insects accidentally entering their mouths.

Southern Asia

Southern Asia is one of the most heavily populated regions of the world – home to more than 20 per cent of the human race. In the north are the towering peaks of the Himalayas. Their foothills sweep down to the crowded, hot, fertile plains around the Indus and Ganges.

❖ The land
The highest peak in southern Asia, and the world, is Everest on the Nepalese/Chinese border at 8848 m. The longest river is the Indus (2900 km).

❖ Climate
The mountains are cool, but much of southern Asia is hot. In summer, temperatures rise well above 30°C in places. The monsoon season brings welcome water.

❖ Population
India 997 m; Pakistan 134 m; Bangladesh 127 m; Burma (Myanmar) 45 m; Sri Lanka 19 m; Nepal 23.3 m; Bhutan 0.8 m.

❖ Capitals
See the map.

❖ Natural resources
Southern Asia is not especially rich in mineral resources, except for precious gems. India has iron ore and coal, as well as mica, manganese and diamonds. Burma (Myanmar) earns a great deal of money from its oil and gas, and is famous for its rubies. Kashmir is known for its blue sapphires.

❖ Farming
Poor soil and lack of water in places has always hampered farming in southern Asia. Nonetheless, two-thirds of people grow their own food. India is the world's second-biggest grower of rice after China, one of the largest growers of wheat and pulses, and the world's prime source of sugar, bananas, tea, sesame seeds and mangoes. It is also a major source of spices. One of the world's most extensive irrigation systems makes the otherwise dry Punjab in Pakistan very fertile.

❖ Forestry
Rosewood and teak are grown for furniture. Huge numbers of trees are cut down for fuel.

❖ Industry and commerce
Since independence, large investments have been made to help turn India into a major industrial nation. Its big steel industry supplies makers of everything from cars and bikes to jet aeroplanes and space rockets. Textiles, cement and machine tools are also major exports – as they are from Pakistan. But half of India's industrial output comes from traditional home craft industries.

❖ Government
India is the world's largest democracy. In 1971, East Pakistan broke away from West Pakistan to become Bangladesh. Both are democracies, but both have had periods of military rule. Burma (Myanmar) has an oppressive military regime. Bhutan is a feudal kingdom; Nepal now has an elected government.

❖ Religion
India is 84 per cent Hindu. Pakistan and Bangladesh are mostly Muslim; Burma (Myanmar), Sri Lanka, Bhutan and Nepal are mainly Buddhist.

❖ Sport
Hockey is India's national game; cricket is popular in India and Pakistan.

Burma ruby
The best rubies in the world are found in the Mogok region of Burma (Myanmar), where superb gems are found in beds of calcite. Even if they do not actually come from Burma, good rubies are referred to as Burma rubies. Some people here believe that wearing a ruby protects you from harm.

Poppy daze
Made from poppy seeds, the drug opium has been used in southern Asia for thousands of years. Opium is used to make the painkiller morphine, but it can also be used to make the drug heroin. Growing opium poppies is one of the few ways the hill people of northern Burma (Myanmar) can make money.

Taj Mahal
Set on the banks of the Yamuna River at Agra is one of the world's most beautiful tombs, the Taj Mahal. Made of jewel-encrusted white marble, it was built by 20,000 workers between 1631 and 1659 for Shah Jahan who wanted it to commemorate his beloved wife, Mumtaz Mahal.

The forest habitat of the tiger in, for example, lowland Nepal, is dwindling rapidly because of tree felling and climatic change.

Keep it colourful
Not only buses, but rickshaws and lorries in Pakistan are decorated with colourful patterns, religious sayings, pictures of film stars, and even landscape paintings. Every little bit of the vehicle is painted. Many people believe that the more beautiful the vehicle is, the more careful the driver will be.

Miles
0   100   200   300   400

Kilometres
0   200   400   600

HINDU KUSH

KARAKORAM RANGE
K2 8611m

HIMALAYA
Mt Everest 8848m
Kanchenjunga 8586m

SULAIMAN RANGE

KIRTHAR RANGE

THAR DESERT

C H I N A

N E P A L

B H U T A N

P A K I S T A N

BANGLADESH

BURMA

NAGA HILLS

CHIN HILLS

Khyber Pass

Peshawar
ISLAMABAD
Rawalpindi
Gujranwala
Faisalabad
Lahore
Multan
Ludhiana
Delhi
NEW DELHI
Jaipur
Ahmadabad
Indore
Bhopal
Kanpur
Lucknow
Varanasi
KATHMANDU
THIMPHU
DHAKA
Karachi
Hyderabad

Indus
Sutlej
Yamuna
Ganges
Ghagara
Son
Narmada
Brahmaputra

Gulf of Kutch

Tropic of Cancer

RUSSIA
KAZAKHSTAN
MONGOLIA
CHINA
NORTH KOREA
SOUTH KOREA
East China Sea
TAIWAN
South China Sea
VIETNAM
LAOS
BURMA
THAILAND
CAMBODIA
MALAYSIA
NEPAL
BHUTAN
BANGLADESH
INDIA
SRI LANKA
Bay of Bengal
PAKISTAN
AFGHANISTAN
TURKMENISTAN
TAJIKISTAN
KYRGYZSTAN
UZBEKISTAN
IRAN
IRAQ
SYRIA
KUWAIT
SAUDI ARABIA
UNITED ARAB EMIRATES
OMAN
YEMEN
Arabian Sea
INDIAN OCEAN
EGYPT
SUDAN
ERITREA
ETHIOPIA
SOMALIA
UGANDA
KENYA
TANZANIA
MOZAMBIQUE
ZIMBABWE
MADAGASCAR

Did you know? Bhutan is ruled by an absolute monarch, called the Dragon King.

LAOS

THAILAND

Salween

Pegu ○
RANGOON ●
Moulmein ○

Mouths of the Irrawaddy

Buddha's hair
Burma's capital, Rangoon, was turned into a thriving port during the British colonial era in the 19th century. But it has been a centre of Burmese culture ever since the first Shwe Dagon pagoda was built here 2500 years ago to house eight sacred hairs of the Buddha. The current pagoda has a spire 100 m high covered in gold and encrusted with diamonds.

Mouths of the Ganges
Bay of Bengal

Jute economy
Jute is a reed that thrives in hot, wet conditions and it is Bangladesh's most important export. There are more than 70 big jute mills in Bangladesh making rope, sacking and carpet backing for export.

A n d a m a n   S e a

ANDAMAN ISLANDS (to India)

NICOBAR ISLANDS (to India)

Floodlands
Most of Bangladesh is low-lying and flat, so flooding is a regular problem. Every summer, from June to October, the monsoon fills rivers to bursting point, while tropical cyclones can swamp coastal regions with storm surges.

Jumbo power
Elephants have long been used in India as working animals for their immense strength – particularly for shifting big logs with their trunks.

farmers, who rely on this rain, face drought and ruin if the rains are late.

Millions of Indians go to the cinema every week. In villages where there is no cinema, the people simply hang up a white sheet in the street to serve as a screen.

Bollywood
Mumbai is the heart of a film industry producing more than 700 films a year, and making huge stars of their lead actors.

Children at work
Many children in India have to work from a very young age. Some sell things on the street. Some work as domestic servants. But many, especially girls, work in textile factories. Conditions in the factories are often dangerous, but recent attempts to force factories not to employ children have not always been successful, since the children sacked must find even worse jobs – or starve.

D E C C A N

Godavari

EASTERN GHATS

Krishna

Mumbai ○
Pune ○

Hyderabad ○

Bangalore ○
Madras ●

WESTERN GHATS

INDIAN OCEAN

Karachi
Karachi is one of southern Asia's biggest cities, a noisy, energetic thriving port of more than nine million people. It is a major industrial centre.

Cow care
The cow has a very special place in India. For the Hindus, cows are sacred. It is illegal to kill a cow, and they are allowed to roam freely in city streets.

Jaffna ●

SRI LANKA
Kandy ○
COLOMBO ●
Galle ○

Gulf of Mannar

Tea break
Sri Lanka has taken over from India as the largest exporter of tea in the world.

Well cast
The Hindu religion plays a very important part in most Indians' lives. Most men and women still have their marriages arranged by their parents in the traditional Hindu way, and women wear the customary sari. The Hindu caste or class system has no legal basis, but marriages are still generally arranged between members of the same caste.

Wet times
After the long parched days of spring, the monsoon season arrives around the end of May and brings four months or so of much-needed rain. The monsoon rains are often torrential and can bring terrible floods that sweep away crops and even whole villages. But the

Indian snake charmer and cobra.

Green revolution?
Growing food for all the people in India can be a problem. About 40 years ago, Indian farmers began to grow high-yield varieties of rice and wheat. Harvests doubled between 1960 and 1976. India now grows more than enough to feed all its people. But much has to be exported, because high-yield crops demand large amounts of fertilizer and pesticide – expensive extras that can only be paid for with foreign earnings.

The Southern Asians

A huge range of different peoples and cultures are crowded into southern Asia – Hindus and Sikhs, Punjabis and Bengalis, Urdu speakers and Gujarati speakers – with very little room to spare. The millions of poor are among the poorest in the world, the few rich are among the richest. With such differences, it is inevitable that there are tensions. Yet, on the whole, the region is remarkably peaceful, and is slowly beginning to prosper.

Sikh man
Some 750 million Indians are Hindus; 100 million are Muslims; and 49 million are Buddhists, Jains, Christians or Sikhs. The Sikhs believe in one god; their holy shrine is the Golden Temple

in Amritsar in the Punjab. A Sikh man must carry the five signs of his religion: the five k's – kachh (shorts), kara (steel bracelet), kirpan (small dagger), and kes (uncut hair and a beard). He covers his head with a turban, a symbol of purity.

Spice time
Spices are used in just about every dish in India, whether sweet or savoury. Cinnamon, cumin, turmeric, saffron, coriander, ginger, pepper, chilli and cardamom and many others are used to make Indian food richly flavoured. There are also some 1000 varieties of rice.

Did you know? Each year, millions of Hindus bathe in the Ganges to wash away their sins.

57

Missing link

Laos is one of the world's poorest countries, and three-quarters of its people grow food only for themselves. But the discovery of iron and gold, as well as the hydroelectric potential of its rivers, has attracted foreign investors who helped pay for the new Friendship Bridge over the Mekong River. This bridge, opened in 1994, completed the first road link between Thailand and China.

Hill tribespeople, Thailand.

The old man

The orang-utan is a large shaggy ape that now lives only in Sabah in East Malaysia. Orang-utan is Malay for Old Man of the Woods. Sadly, this gentle, intelligent creature is facing a losing battle for survival – partly because its forest home is being destroyed by logging and partly because poachers take the youngsters. There are now homes for orphaned orang-utan babies, but these can help only a few.

Monster flower

In Sabah in East Malaysia, there grows a giant flower up to 3 m across. It is the world's largest flower, but it only blooms every ten years and smells like disgusting rotten meat to attract the flies that pollinate it. It is known as Rafflesia, after Sir Stamford Raffles, the man who founded Singapore.

A Philippines jeepney - see edge of this page.

Map labels

CHINA
BURMA (MYANMAR)
Mekong
HANOI
Luang Prabang
Haiphong
Chiang Mai
LAOS
VIENTIANE
Red
Savannakhet
THAILAND
Da Nang
Nakhon Ratchasima
BANGKOK
VIETNAM
CAMBODIA
Mekong
Nha Trang
PHNOM PENH
Ho Chi Minh City
Gulf of Thailand
Mekong River Delta
ANDAMAN SEA

Luzon
PHILIPPINE SEA
MANILA
SOUTH CHINA SEA
PHILIPPINES
Iloilo
Bacolod
Cebu
Palawan
SULU SEA
Cagayan de Oro
Mindanao
Zamboanga
Davao
PALAU

Miles 0 100 200 300 400 500 600
Kilometres 0 300 600 900

Penang
Ipoh
Medan
KUALA LUMPUR
Johor Baharu
SINGAPORE
BARISAN MOUNTAINS
Sumatra
Padang
Hari
Palembang
JAKARTA
Semarang
Bandung
Java
Surabaya
Bali
Lombok
INDIAN OCEAN

Kuching
Borneo
Kapuas
Pontianak
Samarinda
Barito
Banjarmasin
I N D O N E S I A
JAVA SEA
Ujung Pandang
Sulawesi
FLORES SEA
Sumbawa
Sumba
Flores
Kupang
TIMOR SEA

BANDAR SERI BEGAWAN
△ Kinabalu 4101m
CELEBES SEA
BRUNEI
M A L A Y S I A

MOLUCCA SEA
Halmahera
MOLUCCAS
SERAM SEA
Buru
Seram
Ambon
BANDA SEA
Wetar
Timor
Kepulauan Taninbar
Kepulauan Aru
ARAFURA SEA
Mt Puncak Jay 5040m

2020 Vision

Twenty years ago, Malaysia was an agricultural country, relying mainly on rubber for exports. But it is now one of the world's most rapidly developing economies, thanks to a cheap, highly skilled labour force. A plan called 2020 Vision aims to see it fully developed by the year 2020. Nowhere are the signs of this growth more evident than in the gleaming new skyscrapers of the capital, Kuala Lumpur.

The world's busiest port

Centrally located between Asia and the western world, Singapore is one of the world's busiest ports – if not the busiest. Huge ships tie up here every three minutes night and day.

Dayak

The Dayak of Borneo often live in very long wooden houses – up to 300 m long – raised off the ground on stilts. There can be enough rooms for 50 families in one of these houses, each occupying a single room.

A real dragon

The Komodo dragon is the nearest thing in the world to a real dragon. It is actually a giant lizard which lives on the island of Komodo in Indonesia. But it is very big – up to 3 m long – and very fierce, chasing and eating small deer, wild pigs, water buffalos and even humans.

Stilt houses

Many people live near rivers in Southeast Asia, and there is a constant danger of flooding. As a result, many traditional houses are built on stilts.

FACE THE FACTS...

❖ **The land**
The highest peak in the region is Puncak Jaya in Indonesia (5040 m). On the mainland, it is Mt Kinabalu in Malaysia (4101 m). The longest river is the Mekong in Vietnam (4500 km).

❖ **Climate**
Southeast Asia lies entirely within the tropics and the climate is hot and humid. There is usually a monsoon season and coastal regions are frequently battered by storms called typhoons.

❖ **Population**
Indonesia 205 m; Vietnam 77.5 m; Philippines 74.2 m; Thailand 60 m; Malaysia 22.7 m; Cambodia 11.7 m; Laos 5 m; Singapore 3.9 m; East Timor 920,000; Brunei 322,000.

❖ **Capitals**
See the map.

❖ **Natural resources**
Southeast Asia is rich in tin, oil and natural gas.

❖ **Farming**
Beyond the dense forests, this is one of the most intensively farmed parts of the world. Every available space is used for growing rice, especially, but also sugar cane, tobacco, cassava, tea, coffee, spices and palm oil. Coconuts are gathered from palm trees near the coast, while inland trees are tapped for rubber. In Thailand, silkworm caterpillars are reared to make silk.

❖ **Forestry**
In much of Southeast Asia, logging has been reduced to protect the rainforest.

❖ **Industry and commerce**
Most of Southeast Asia's people earn their living from farming, but industry is growing rapidly in Malaysia and Singapore. Malaysia is a world leader in electronics.

❖ **Government**
Laos, Cambodia and Vietnam were all caught up in the bitter struggles between the communists and their opponents in the 1960s and 1970s, and millions of Cambodians died under the military dictatorship of Pol Pot. Laos and Vietnam are now both communist republics, while Cambodia has restored its king. Thailand is a monarchy. Democracy was restored in the Philippines in 1986, while Indonesia held multi-party elections in 1999. East Timor broke away from Indonesia in 2002.

❖ **Religion**
Cambodia, Vietnam, Thailand and Burma are mainly Buddhist; Indonesia and Malaysia are Muslim.

❖ **Sport**
Soccer is popular in Indonesia. In Thailand, the national sport is Thai boxing.

Southeast Asia

Southeast Asia is a region of mountains and forests, islands and wide plains watered by broad rivers. The warm, damp climate fosters fertile lands and one of the densest rural populations in the world. Today, some countries, such as Malaysia, are thriving on new industries in high-tech modern cities. Others, such as Cambodia, are still trying to live with the scars of some of the most terrible wars in recent history.

Rice everywhere
Half of all the cultivated land in Southeast Asia is used for growing rice. Flooded paddy fields cover every river plain, and ancient terraces climb up every spare hillside. The fields are ploughed by water buffalo and then flooded for the rice to be planted by hand.

The Southeast Asians

There is an incredibly rich variety of peoples and cultures in Southeast Asia. There are over 250 different languages spoken in Indonesia. Each of these peoples has its own distinctive history and way of life. Some Southeast Asians, such as those in Singapore and Kuala Lumpur, have embraced modern Western lifestyles; others are facing the loss of their culture as economic pressures – sometimes backed up by brute force – drive them from their traditional homes.

Striking it rich
Oil has made the tiny country of Brunei one of the world's richest. Taxes on oil exports bring in so much money that the people of Brunei get free education and healthcare without paying any taxes. The Sultan of Brunei is probably the world's richest man with an estimated fortune of $37 billion.

Forest catastrophe
Indonesia has one of the few large remaining areas of rainforest in the world, with all its rich diversity of life. Yet an area the size of Wales is cut or simply burned down every year. In 1997, loggers carelessly set alight vast areas of the forest. The flames covered much of Indonesia with choking smoke that meant that children had to wear face masks to school.

Thai food
Food in Thailand is very spicy. As with most of Southeast Asia, rice and fish are the basic ingredients, and to these are added lemongrass, chillies, coriander and coconut or flavouring. Popular dishes include tom-yam-gung (a spicy soup), fried fish, and pat preeowahn (shrimps fried with pineapple, garlic, cucumbers, tomatoes and onions). The Thais also like to eat lots of fruit and drink cold lemon tea or iced sugar-cane juice.

FACE THE FACTS...

❖ The land

The highest mountain in China (and the world) is Qomolanjma (Mt. Everest, 8848 m) on the Chinese-Nepalese border. The longest river is the Chang (Yangtze) (6300 km).

country; the far north is very cold while the south is tropical. The extremes of the interior are summed up by the Chinese saying, 'a fur-lined jacket at dawn, a gauze shirt at noon'.

❖ Population

China's population is 1.23 billion; 22 m live in Taiwan; 2.3 m in Mongolia; 23 m in North Korea and 46.8 m in South Korea.

❖ Climate

The typical Chinese climate is continental monsoon.
But it is a very big

❖ Capitals

See the map.

enough food to feed them all. The major crop in the hot and humid south is rice, grown in flooded paddy fields by the Chang (Yangtze) and Huang (Yellow) Rivers, but tea, sugar, cotton, fruit and vegetables are also grown here. In the north, wheat is grown and many farmers tend sheep and cattle. On the vast pastures of Mongolia, they herd cattle, yaks, sheep and goats.

❖ Natural resources

China has a rich range of resources including coal, iron ore, tungsten, tin, antimony and wolfram, although many of these are in remote, inaccessible places. Oil is produced in northern provinces such as Shandong and Heilongjiang, and offshore fields are being developed.

❖ Farming

Seventy per cent of China's huge population still live in the country, where the fertile soils provide

❖ Industry and commerce

Not long ago China was essentially an agricultural

country. But heavy industry is developing rapidly.

❖ Government

China is a communist country. It has an elected parliament called the National People's Congress, headed by a president, but it is under the control of the Communist Party leadership. The General Secretary of the party is also the Chinese president.

❖ Religion

There is no official religion in China, but Buddhism, Taoism

and Confucianism are widely practised.

❖ Language

Most people in China speak Chinese, but there are many different dialects, and people who speak one, such as Mandarin, will not necessarily understand someone who speaks another.

❖ Sport

The Chinese are good at badminton, volleyball, gymnastics and, especially, table tennis, often played on makeshift stone tables.

Northeast Asia

China dominates this region: it is the most populous country in the world, home to one in every five people alive today. It is a huge and varied country – the third largest in the world – stretching from the lofty Himalayas in the west to the vast empty Gobi desert in the north and the fertile plains of the great Chang (Yangtze) and Huang (Yellow) Rivers where most Chinese people live.

Riders of the north

The best way to get around the vast grassy plains of Mongolia is on horseback, and many Mongols are superb riders. They learn to ride very early. Boys and girls as young as five get a chance to display their prowess at the races.

The Great Wall

Snaking for more than 6700 km across northern China, the Great Wall is said to be the only man-made structure that can be seen from space by day. It was first built around 210 BC to protect against nomadic invaders.

Junk

The distinctive flat-bottomed wooden boats called junks have been used for well over a thousand years. Huge sailing junks like floating castles were being used to sail around China centuries before such large ships were ever dreamed of in Europe.

Korea economy

In 1948, Korea split into communist North and capitalist South – and a bitter war was fought between the two. After the war, money from American banks helped South Korea become the world's fastest growing economy. Huge new factories run by companies called *chaebol* churned out everything from computers to cars such as the Hyundai.

Korean ships

South Korea's giant shipyards build one in six of the world's ships. Only Japan builds more.

Map labels:
Sea of Okhotsk
Amur
RUSSIA
Manchurian Plain
DA HINGGAN LING
Qiqihar
Harbin
Jilin
Changchun
Fushun
Shenyang
Anshan
Dalian
Tangshan
Chongjin
Sinuiju
NORTH KOREA
PYONGYANG
Nampo
Inchon
SEOUL
SOUTH KOREA
Taegu
Pusan
Sea of Japan
Yellow Sea
Tianjin
Zibo
Qingdao
Jinan
Shijiazhuang
Taiyuan
BEIJING
Datong
Baotou
ULAN BATOR
MONGOLIA
Hövsgöl Nuur
Gobi Desert
Huang
QILIAN SHAN
ALTAI MOUNTAINS
Ürümqi
TIAN SHAN
TAKLIMAKAN DESERT
KYRGYZSTAN
TAJIKISTAN

Globe map labels:
Sea of Okhotsk
RUSSIA
MONGOLIA
NORTH KOREA
SOUTH KOREA
JAPAN
Sea of Japan
Yellow Sea
East China Sea
CHINA
TAIWAN
VIETNAM
LAOS
BURMA
THAILAND
CAMBODIA
South China Sea
NEPAL
BHUTAN
BANGLADESH
INDIA
SRI LANKA
Bay of Bengal
PAKISTAN
AFGHANISTAN
IRAN
OMAN
TURKMENISTAN
UZBEKISTAN
TAJIKISTAN
KYRGYZSTAN
KAZAKHSTAN
INDIAN OCEAN

Did you know? In the northwest, many people live in homes dug out of the soft powdery rock, complete with electricity.

Grand Canal
China's Grand Canal is the longest and oldest man-made waterway in the world, 1800 km from end to end and first constructed as early as the 5th century BC – much the same time as Ancient Athens was flourishing in Europe.

Cloth in Canton
Guangzhou (Canton) is one of the fastest growing cities in China, and now that Hong Kong is part of China too, this area will probably become a focus for industrial development.

Hong Kong
Packed on to hilly islands off the coast of mainland China, Hong Kong is one of the world's most crowded, bustling, dynamic cities. For 155 years, it was ruled by the British and made itself rich through energetic trading and industry. It was returned to China in 1997.

Banned in Tibet
Tibet is spread out over the highest plateau in the world – averaging over 4000 m high, only a little lower than the loftiest peaks in the European Alps. Ever since the Chinese took over the country in the 1950s, they have tried to discourage Buddhism, once the main religion in Tibet. In 1950, there were some 6000 Buddhist monasteries in Tibet. By 1978, there were just 13.

Pedal power
Hundreds of millions of Chinese people travel by bike, or by bus and train, because few can afford cars.

Giant panda
The giant panda is one of the world's rarest creatures. It lives only in small, remote areas of western Szechwan and eastern Sikang where steep-sided mountains grow thick with dripping bamboo forests. It looks like a bear but is in fact a raccoon and feeds on rare types of bamboo shoot.

Shimmering lands
Every bit of fertile land in China is farmed, and in the cities, terrace after terrace of rice paddy fields climb up even the steepest hillside. Paddy fields are surrounded by mudbanks that keep them flooded while the new rice is growing. Women plant out the new shoots by hand twice a year.

Limestone peaks
Near Guilin in southern China, spectacular limestone pillars rise from the flooded paddies of the plains. Steep-sided and covered with hanging trees, they were made by the slow corrosion of the limestone as rainwater trickled through the ground over millions of years. Inside the hills, spectacular mazes of caves have formed.

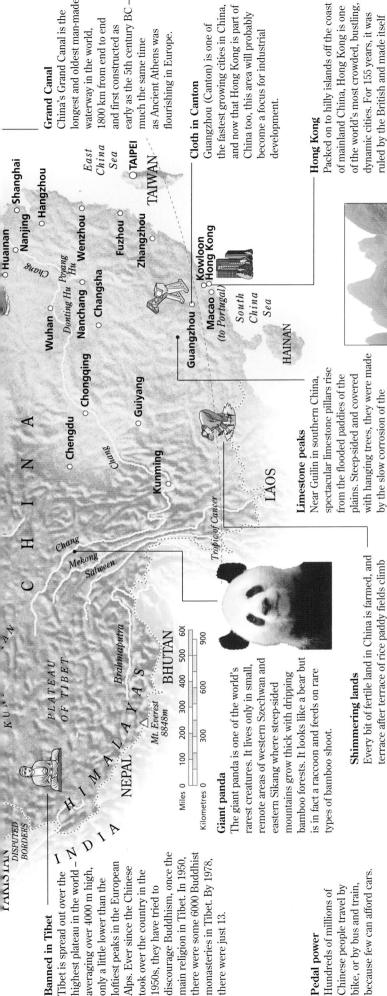

The Chinese
In recent years, China has opened up to Western influences and, in the cities, many Chinese people have adopted aspects of the Western lifestyle. Still, the vast majority of Chinese live in the country in a way that has changed little for centuries, with large families – grandparents, cousins, aunts and uncles – all living together in small houses and working hard in the fields.

Country life
In the country, Chinese farmers get up at the crack of dawn, eat a bowl of rice porridge and vegetables and go out to the fields until nightfall. In the evening, they might have the same food, eaten with chopsticks, often by oil- or candle-light, for many houses are without electricity.

All the tea
The Chinese were drinking tea at least 4000 years ago. They drink it without milk – green, black or scented. Most tea is made from jasmine, but oolong and chrysanthemum are popular too.

Trendsetting
With so many people, China is a potentially vast market for American and European businesses. Most of the country is still closed to them, but in big cities such as Beijing things are changing. Many rich young Chinese are now listening to Western pop music and buying Western fashions. Beijing even has shops selling clothes by top European designers, such as Armani, but these are far too expensive for most Chinese.

Tiananmen Square
Beijing's Tiananmen Square is the biggest city square in the world – a vast open space built to celebrate the People's Republic. In 1989, students gathered here to press the government for a little more freedom. But the protest ended in tragedy as troops opened fire, killing hundreds of young people. Many survivors were arrested and others were forced into hiding.

Ancient remedies
Although China uses modern surgical and drug treatments, it has its own tradition of medicine dating back thousands of years. Chinese chemists sell a wide range of herbal remedies, while many people are treated by acupuncture, an ancient healing system that involves sticking needles into the skin at carefully selected points.

Little Emperors
China's population was growing so rapidly – by about 15 million people a year – that in 1979, the government made it illegal for parents to have more than one child. This policy worked well in towns, where the single children are known as *Little Emperors* because they are often spoiled. It worked less well in the country where extra children were needed to work in the fields. At one time, it was feared girl babies were being hidden or even murdered so that a family's one child could be a boy.

Left, traditional Korean dance; above right, Chinese food and chopsticks

PAKISTAN
DISPUTED BORDERS

KUN LUN

PLATEAU OF TIBET

Mt. Everest 8848m

HIMALAYAS

NEPAL

BHUTAN

INDIA

Brahmaputra

Chang

Mekong

Salween

CHINA

Chengdu

Chongqing

Kunming

Guiyang

Tropic of Cancer

LAOS

Wuhan

Changsha

Nanchang

Dongting Hu

Poyang Hu

Wenzhou

Fuzhou

Zhangzhou

Guangzhou

Macao (to Portugal)

Kowloon
Hong Kong

HAINAN

South China Sea

TAIWAN

○ TAIPEI

East China Sea

Shanghai

Hangzhou

Nanjing

Huainan

Chang

Miles 0   100   200   300   400   500   600

Kilometres 0   300   600   900

Did you know? Chinese athletes eat the caterpillar fungus, which grows from dead caterpillar bodies, to improve their speed.

Did you know? Winters in Hokkaido are so cold, that every winter people carve fabulous giant ice sculptures in the streets.

FACE THE FACTS...

❖ **Land**
Japan's highest mountain is Mt Fujiyama (3776 m), also known as Mount Fuji – see the map. Its longest river is the Shinano-gawa (370 km).

❖ **Climate**
Summers are hot throughout the country, but winters in the north can be bitterly cold. Monsoon rains and typhoons hit the south in summer.

❖ **Population**
Some 126 million people live in Japan, mostly on the islands of Honshu and Kyushu.

❖ **Capital**
Japan's capital is Tokyo, one of the biggest cities in the world.

❖ **Resources**
Japan has few natural mineral resources so it imports oil and iron ore.

❖ **Farming**
All but 15 per cent of the land is too steep for farming, but hillsides are terraced to give extra flat land. The main crops are rice, along with vegetables, soya beans, barley and wheat.

❖ **Fishing**
The Japanese catch a huge amount of fish – and whales too.

❖ **Industry & commerce**
Japan is famous for its electronic goods – the Sony Walkman was invented by the Japanese Sony company in the 1970s, and Japan is the home of the Nintendo, too. It also makes a great deal of the world's steel, half of the world's ships and more cars than any other country.

❖ **Government**
For centuries Japan was ruled by an all-powerful emperor. There is still an emperor and an imperial family, but since World War II, Japan has been run by an elected parliament.

❖ **Currency**
The Japanese pay for things in yen. Although the Japanese have used paper money longer than anyone, the yen they use today originated with the old silver dollars once used by American traders.

❖ **Religion**
Most Japanese belong to the Buddhist or Shinto religions, but many still follow the advice of the ancient Chinese wise man, Confucius.

❖ **Sport**
The national sport is Sumo wrestling in which two really overweight men try to push each other out of the ring.

Japan

Japan is made up of four large islands – Hokkaido, Honshu, Shikoku and Kyushu – and almost 4000 smaller ones. It is a very mountainous land, with steep forested slopes and fast-flowing rivers. Most Japanese people live in the narrow plains by the sea or along river valleys.

Shrines and temples
Japan has many old Buddhist temples with graceful upcurved roofs, and old wooden Shinto shrines. They are often set in beautiful landscaped gardens, as the Japanese have a deep respect for nature.

Bullet train
Japan's famous bullet train or Shinkansen was the world's first 200 km/h train, and now speeds passengers over 1,170 km from Tokyo to Fukuoka in under six hours – going through the world's longest railway tunnel under the sea to Hokkaido en route.

Fish
The seas around Japan's long and intricate coast are home to the world's largest fishing industry. More than 400,000 fishing vessels put out their nets to catch over 12 million tonnes of fish a year – and fish are becoming much scarcer in the once teeming seas. The Japanese have also resisted pressure to stop hunting whales, and Japanese whalers still catch hundreds of minke whales every year.

Farmers
Japan's farmland is shrinking as its cities grow, but there are still millions of little square rice-fields packed into the narrow coastal plain. Japanese farms tend to be very small and are often worked by elderly people or those who have other jobs in the city as well.

Pine tree
The Japanese love the twisted shape of the pine tree. It is a typical sight in the Japanese countryside, especially by the coast.

KURIL ISLANDS (to RUSSIA)

La Pérouse Strait

RISHIRI ISLANDS

Hokkaido

HIDAKA MOUNTAINS

Sapporo

Tsugaru Strait

Honshu

Sendai

SADO

JAPAN

SEA OF JAPAN

Miles
Kilometres

Bering Sea

Sea of Okhotsk

PACIFIC OCEAN

RUSSIA

Sea of Japan

JAPAN

NORTH KOREA

SOUTH KOREA

Yellow Sea

East China Sea

Philippine Sea

TAIWAN

HONG KONG

South China Sea

CHINA

MONGOLIA

Big cities, crowded living
Because Japan is so mountainous, the big cities, where nine out of ten Japanese people live, are crowded along the coastal plains. Over 40 million people live in Tokyo and its suburbs, crammed into tiny flats.

Skyscrapers
Tokyo has some of the world's most spectacular new buildings, soaring to great heights to make maximum use of the limited space. Architects are now planning a building over 1000 m high.

Mount Fuji
The most famous of Japan's 2000 volcanoes is the beautiful snow-capped Mt Fujiyama – inspiration for poets and painters since earliest times. Fuji is sacred to the Shinto religion and each year many thousands of pilgrims ascend the shrine-bordered paths leading to the summit.

Kansai
There is so little spare land in Japan that the futuristic airport of Kansai was built on a specially created artificial island in Osaka Bay. It includes an extraordinary conveyor belt that can whisk some 44,000 passengers a day to and from aircraft.

Steel city
The city of Kita kyushu on Kyushu island has long been the focus of the Japanese iron and steel industry. Now it is the home to the Nippon Steel Corporation, the world's largest steel company, and the Corporation's gigantic steelworks in the Kita kyushu industrial complex produces millions of tonnes of steel every year.

Earthquakes
Japanese cities are frequently rocked by earthquakes, so new office buildings are built to withstand quite severe shocks. Yet this did not stop the devastation of the city of Kobe in 1995, when many died.

Banded sea snake
This dangerous snake, with a tail flattened to make a paddle, lives in the sea around Japan. Its bite is more poisonous than any other snake's.

Rice and fish
Fish is the people's main food, because there is so little farmland. They often eat it raw in thin slices called sashimi or cooked with batter and vegetables in tempura. Most Japanese also eat a lot of boiled rice and noodles. They eat using chopsticks (not knives and forks), as they have always done. It is a healthy diet.

Sushi, a Japanese speciality

dress in fabulous costumes and heavy mask-like make-up and tell poetic stories in ritual mime, music and strange voices.

Silk and paper
Most Japanese children wear western-style dress at school or when out playing. But on special occasions, Japanese girls often wear beautiful traditional hand-embroidered silk kimonos (gowns), tied with a sash, and carry a painted waxed paper umbrella.

Low tables
Traditional Japanese houses had paper walls and hardly any furniture except for knee-high tables and cushions. Even though they now live mainly in western style flats, Japanese people have their main meal around the same low tables.

Noh way
The Noh is a very old and sacred form of theatre. Men

alphabet. Words are usually spelled out in a mixture of kanji and hiragana or katakana symbols.

Japanese flag
The Japanese call their country Nippon, which means source of the sun, because people all along the east coast see the sun rise far out across the Pacific. The flag is a red rising sun against a white background.

Japanese writing
In Japanese writing, words are shown by one of thousands of 'kanji' symbols, which are like little pictures with a particular meaning. But there are also 46 'hiragana', and 46 'katakana' symbols, each representing a different sound such as 'ka' or 'me', like the letters of our

The Japanese
Most Japanese homes are very modern and full of electronic gadgets, but the Japanese take great pride in their traditional culture and religion. Many Japanese children go out to play baseball and eat fast food, then go home for tea ceremonies (dress: kimono) – or they practise karate.

Cat *Flower*

Did you know? One of the world's first novels, written as early as 1100, was in Japanese.

Africa

Africa is the world's second largest continent, stretching 8000 km from the Mediterranean in the north to the Cape of Good Hope in the south. It is also the warmest, for the equator runs right through the middle, and temperatures in the Sahara desert are the highest on Earth.

Most of the continent is an immense plateau, broken here and there by mountain ranges such as Uganda's Ruwenzori and in the east by the deep gorge of the Great Rift Valley – features described and shown on the detailed map on page 68. Along the tropics lie two vast deserts, the Kalahari in the south and the Sahara in the north. In the west and centre there are lush rainforests. Much of the rest of Africa is savannah grassland and bush.

Africa has been inhabited by humans far longer than anywhere else in the world. The oldest remains of hominids (human-like creatures), dating from 3.5 million years ago, are the Australopithecines found in the Olduvai Gorge in Tanzania, which has proved an especially rich source. The most famous Australopithecine of all, dubbed 'Lucy', was found in Hadar in Ethiopia in the 1970s.

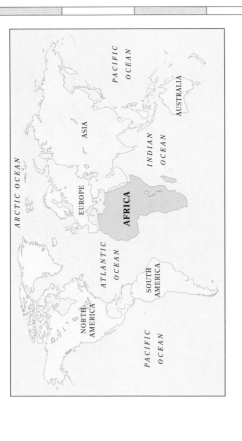

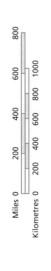

Miles 0   200   400   600   800
Kilometres 0   200   400   600   800   1000

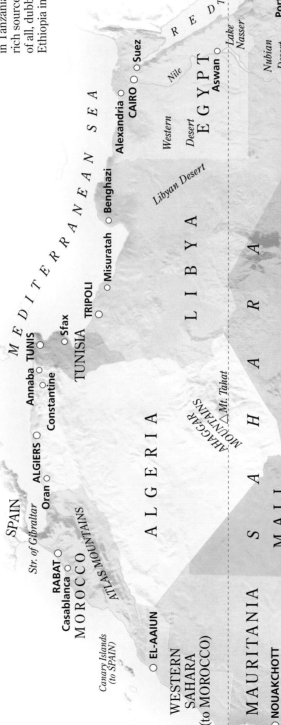

ATLANTIC OCEAN

INDIAN OCEAN

GULF OF GUINEA

SOMALIA
○ MOGADISHU
Equator
○ Kismayu

○ BANGUI

UGANDA KENYA
KAMPALA ○ Kisumu
○ Mombasa
Lake Victoria
Mt. Kenya △
NAIROBI ○
Kilimanjaro △
○ Zanzibar
○ Dar-es-Salaam
DODOMA ○
Rufiji
TANZANIA
○ Kisangani
CONGO
RWANDA ○ KIGALI
○ Mwanza
BUJUMBURA ○ BURUNDI
Lake Tanganyika
Lake Mweru
Congo
CONGO (DEMOCRATIC) REPUBLIC
○ KINSHASA
BRAZZAVILLE ○

COMOROS
Antisiranana ○
○ Mahajanga
ANTANANARIVO ○
MADAGASCAR
Fianarantsoa ○
Mozambique Channel
Tropic of Capricorn

Lake Nyasa
MALAWI
LILONGWE ○
○ Blantyre
○ Beira
MOZAMBIQUE
Zambezi
○ HARARE
ZIMBABWE
○ Bulawayo
Limpopo
○ MAPUTO
○ MBABANE
SWAZILAND
○ Durban
○ East London
○ Port Elizabeth

Lubumbashi ○
Ndola ○
ZAMBIA
LUSAKA ○
Livingstone ○
Okavango Basin
BOTSWANA
GABORONE ○
Kalahari Desert
PRETORIA ○
Johannesburg ○
LESOTHO
MASERU ○
DRAKENSBERG
SOUTH AFRICA
Cape Town ○
Cape of Good Hope

MALABO ○
EQUATORIAL GUINEA
○ YAOUNDÉ
○ LIBREVILLE
SÃO TOMÉ & PRINCIPE
GABON
CONGO
LUANDA ○
ANGOLA PLATEAU
Lobito ○
○ Huambo
ANGOLA
Okavango
Okavango
NAMIBIA
WINDHOEK ○
Namib Desert
Orange

Many remarkable cultures have come and gone on the African continent, including those of Ancient Egypt, Mali and Zimbabwe; and in today's Africa, there is also an enormous variety of cultures. In the north, in countries such as Algeria, Morocco and Egypt, people are mainly Arabic. To the south, people are mostly black Africans, but there are 800 different ethnic groups, each with its own culture and lifestyle. In fact, 1300 languages are spoken in Africa, more than in any other continent.

Much of Africa is so hot and dry, and the soil so thin, that in many places people have always led a nomadic or semi-nomadic lifestyle. Some are forever on the move with their herds, looking for fresh pasture. Others clear away trees and grow crops for a few years, then leave the land to recover. Only in the north – in the Nile Valley and the fertile coast – and in the far south, is most of the land more permanently settled.

Until quite recently, most of Africa's people lived in the countryside in small hut villages, much as they have for thousands of years. Most Africans still grow food for themselves – cassava, yams and bananas in wetter areas, corn in drier areas. But, as more and more land has been taken up for cash crops such as coffee, cocoa and palm-oil, millions of Africans have headed for growing cities such as Cairo in Egypt and Abidjan on the Ivory Coast. The use of all this land for cash crops has also left much less room for shifting cultivation, so farmers are forced, more and more, to stay in one place. As a result, the soil becomes exhausted and crop yields fall. This is one reason why many people in Africa have become very poor.

In the 1980s, the effects of war and overuse of land were made worse by a series of droughts. People in Ethiopia, Sudan, Somalia and Mozambique in particular suffered terrible famines. The worst of these famines is over now, but the line between survival and starvation remains tenuous for many Africans.

Despite the problems they have suffered, many African countries are beginning to put the troubles of the post-colonial years behind them and to thrive for the first time.

Northern Africa

Dominating the centre of northern Africa is the huge, dry, empty expanse of the Sahara. To the north, fringing the Mediterranean, are the Muslim countries with their ancient towns and villages. The southern fringes of the desert form the dusty scrub of the Sahel, where nomadic herders are continually threatened by drought. Further south still are the dense, green rainforests of West Africa.

FACT THE FACTS...

❖ Land

Highest points include Ras Dashen in Ethiopia (4620 m) and Toubkal in Morocco (4165 m). Longest rivers: the Nile (6738 km) and the Niger (4100 km).

❖ Climate

Most of northern Africa is very warm indeed. The northern coast has a Mediterranean climate. In the centre is the Sahara, the world's biggest desert. Dallol, Ethiopia, is the world's hottest place, averaging 34.4°C.

❖ Population

Largest in the region are Nigeria 123.9 m; Egypt 62.6 m; Algeria 29.9 m; Ethiopia 62.7 m; Sudan 29 m; Morocco 28.2 m; Ghana 18.7 m; Ivory Coast 15.5 m; Cameroon 14.6 m; Burkina Faso 11 m; Mali 10.5 m; Niger 10.4 m. The rest generally have populations under 10 million, for example Somalia 9.4 m; Tunisia 9.4 m; Senegal 9.2 m; Chad 7.4 m; Guinea 7.2 m. Gambia has 1.2 m and Djibouti 648,000.

❖ Capitals

See the map.

❖ Natural resources

Algeria, Egypt, Libya, Tunisia, and, especially, Nigeria have huge oil and gas reserves which have helped make them relatively wealthy. Guinea is the world's second largest producer of bauxite (aluminium ore). Morocco and Tunisia have most of the world's phosphate. Uranium is Niger's main export. Ghana and Liberia export gold and diamonds.

❖ Agriculture

Huge areas are unsuitable for farming. In the north crops are 'Mediterranean' – olives, grapes and oranges. In Egypt, Sudan and other countries across the centre, vast amounts of cotton are grown. In West Africa, peanuts are grown on huge plantations; also cocoa beans, coffee, palm oil and rubber and basic tropical crops, such as rice and cassava.

❖ Forestry

The forests of West Africa have been much exploited for hardwoods. Production is down as easy-to-reach wood runs out.

❖ Industry

Manufacturing industry is concentrated mainly on the north coast, in, for example, Morocco, Algeria, Tunisia and Egypt, and in cities such as Lagos in Nigeria.

❖ Government

Many countries have unstable or European-style governments. Many West African countries have returned to multi-party systems.

❖ Religion

In the north, Muslim. Further south, a mixture of Muslim, Christian and traditional beliefs.

❖ Sport

Various, including football.

Marrakech

Situated at the foot of the Atlas Mountains in Morocco is the ancient Arab city of Marrakech, dominated by the minaret (tower) of the Koutoubya mosque. Thousands of tourists come here every year to wander through its narrow streets and haggle for beautiful hand-woven carpets, leather goods and much more in the city's famous souk, or market.

Marrakech carpet trader.

Pyramids

On the edge of the Libyan desert near Cairo are the awesome pyramids, the vast tombs built for the pharaohs (kings) of Ancient Egypt more than 4,000 years ago. The most famous of these is the 147-m-high Great Pyramid of Cheops at Giza built in 2,680 BC. Egypt relies heavily on the thousands of tourists who come here to see the ancient sites – but terrorist attacks by Muslim extremists have scared many away.

Suez canal

Completed in 1869 under the guidance of French entrepreneur Ferdinand de Lesseps (1805–94), the Suez Canal links the Mediterranean with the Red Sea. In doing so it saves ships that sail between Europe and Asia from going all the way round Africa and so cuts thousands of kilometres off the journey.

Miles
0
100
200
300
400
500
600

Kilometres
0
200
400
600
800

MEDITERRANEAN SEA

SPAIN
Strait of Gibraltar
MOROCCO
RABAT
Casablanca
Fez
Oujda
Oran
ALGIERS
Annaba
Constantine
TUNIS
TUNISIA
Sfax
TRIPOLI
Misurata
Gulf of Sidra
Derna
Benghazi
LIBYA
LIBYAN DESERT
Alexandria
CAIRO
Port Said
Suez
JORDAN
SAUDI
Arabian Desert
Nile
WESTERN DESERT
ALGERIA
AHAGGAR MOUNTAINS
Marrakech
Toubkal 4165m
ATLAS MOUNTAINS
CANARY ISLANDS (to SPAIN)
Madeira (to PORTUGAL)
EL-AAIUN
WESTERN SAHARA

ATLANTIC OCEAN
SOUTH AMERICA
POLAND
UKRAINE
RUSSIA
KAZAKHSTAN
CHINA
ITALY
GREECE
TURKEY
SYRIA
IRAN
PAKISTAN
INDIA
Mediterranean Sea
SPAIN
MOROCCO
WESTERN SAHARA
MAURITANIA
MALI
ALGERIA
LIBYA
TUNISIA
NIGER
CHAD
SUDAN
EGYPT
SAUDI ARABIA
OMAN
YEMEN
ERITREA
ETHIOPIA
SOMALIA
DJIBOUTI
CENTRAL AFRICAN REPUBLIC
CAMEROON
NIGERIA
GABON
CONGO
ZAIRE
UGANDA
KENYA
TANZANIA
ANGOLA
ZAMBIA
MALAWI
ZIMBABWE
NAMIBIA
BOTSWANA
SOUTH AFRICA
MADAGASCAR
INDIAN OCEAN

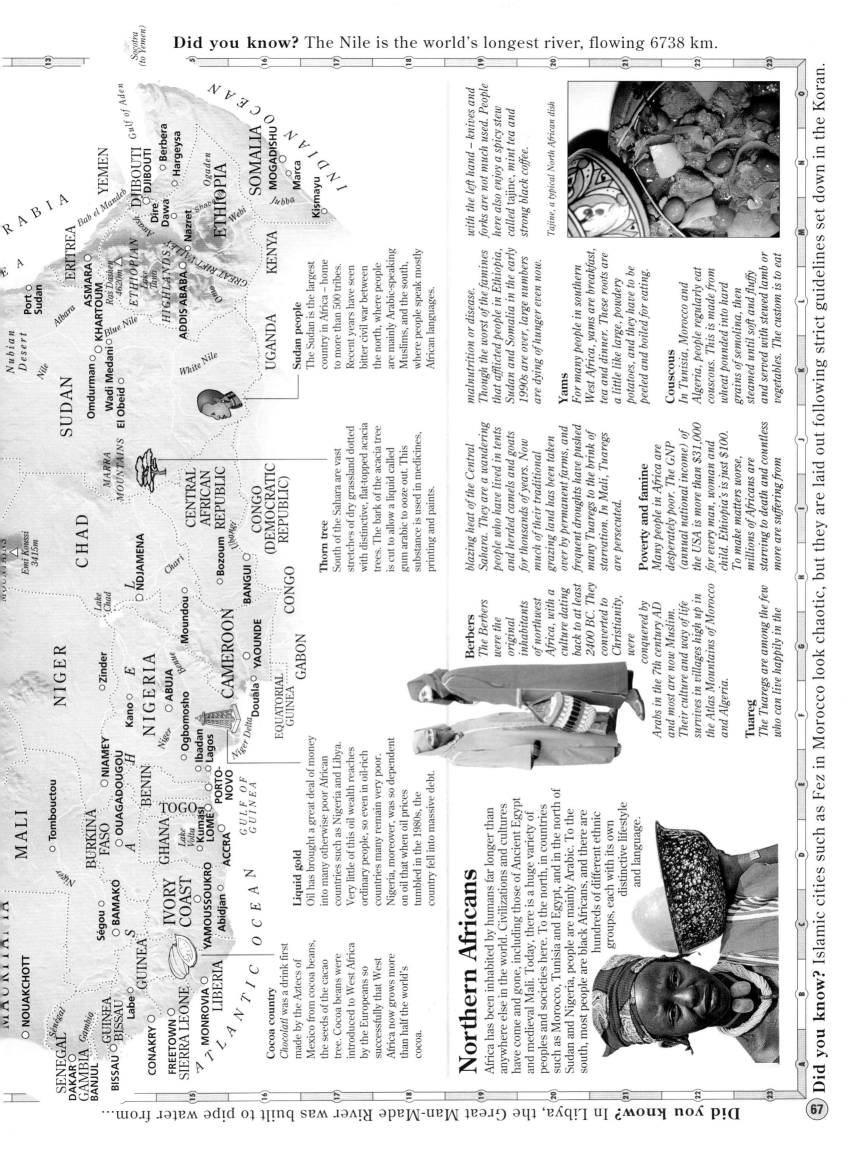

Tajine, a typical North African dish

---

with the left hand – knives and forks are not much used. People here also enjoy a spicy stew called tajine, mint tea and strong black coffee.

Sudan people
The Sudan is the largest country in Africa – home to more than 500 tribes. Recent years have seen bitter civil war between the north, where people are mainly Arabic-speaking Muslims, and the south, where people speak mostly African languages.

Thorn tree
South of the Sahara are vast stretches of dry grassland dotted with distinctive, flat-topped acacia trees. The bark of the acacia tree is cut to allow a liquid called gum arabic to ooze out. This substance is used in medicines, printing and paints.

Berbers
The Berbers were the original inhabitants of northwest Africa, with a culture dating back to at least 2400 BC. They converted to Christianity, were conquered by Arabs in the 7th century AD and most are now Muslim. Their culture and way of life survives in villages high up in the Atlas Mountains of Morocco and Algeria.

Tuareg
The Tuaregs are among the few who can live happily in the blazing heat of the Central Sahara. They are a wandering people who have lived in tents and herded camels and goats for thousands of years. Now much of their traditional grazing land has been taken over by permanent farms, and frequent droughts have pushed many Tuaregs to the brink of starvation. In Mali, Tuaregs are persecuted.

Poverty and famine
Many people in Africa are desperately poor. The GNP (annual national income) of the USA is more than $31,000 for every man, woman and child. Ethiopia's is just $100. To make matters worse, millions of Africans are starving to death and countless more are suffering from malnutrition or disease. Though the worst of the famines that afflicted people in Ethiopia, Sudan and Somalia in the early 1990s are over, large numbers are dying of hunger even now.

Yams
For many people in southern West Africa, yams are breakfast, tea and dinner. These roots are a little like large, powdery potatoes, and they have to be peeled and boiled for eating.

Couscous
In Tunisia, Morocco and Algeria, people regularly eat couscous. This is made from wheat pounded into hard grains of semolina, then steamed until soft and fluffy and served with stewed lamb or vegetables. The custom is to eat

---

Northern Africans

Africa has been inhabited by humans far longer than anywhere else in the world. Civilizations and cultures have come and gone, including those of Ancient Egypt and medieval Mali. Today, there is a huge variety of peoples and societies here. To the north, in countries such as Morocco, Tunisia and Egypt, and in the north of Sudan and Nigeria, people are mainly Arabic. To the south, most people are black Africans, and there are hundreds of different ethnic groups, each with its own distinctive lifestyle and language.

Liquid gold
Oil has brought a great deal of money into many otherwise poor African countries such as Nigeria and Libya. Very little of this oil wealth reaches ordinary people, so even in oil-rich countries many remain very poor. Nigeria, moreover, was so dependent on oil that when oil prices tumbled in the 1980s, the country fell into massive debt.

Cocoa country
Chocolatl was a drink first made by the Aztecs of Mexico from cocoa beans, the seeds of the cacao tree. Cocoa beans were introduced to West Africa by the Europeans so successfully that West Africa now grows more than half the world's cocoa.

Did you know? Islamic cities such as Fez in Morocco look chaotic, but they are laid out following strict guidelines set down in the Koran.

Map labels

ARABIA
YEMEN
Socotra (to Yemen)
Gulf of Aden
Bab el Mandeb
ERITREA
ASMARA
Port Sudan
Omdurman KHARTOUM
Wadi Medani
El Obeid
Nubian Desert
Nile
Atbara
Ràs Dàshen 4620m
Blue Nile
Lake Tana
ETHIOPIAN HIGHLANDS
ADDIS ABABA
White Nile
SUDAN
MARRA MOUNTAINS
CHAD
Emi Koussi 3415m
NIGER
Lake Chad
NDJAMENA
Chari
CENTRAL AFRICAN REPUBLIC
Bozoum
BANGUI
CONGO
CONGO (DEMOCRATIC REPUBLIC)
Ubangi
GABON
YAOUNDE
CAMEROON
EQUATORIAL GUINEA
Douala
GULF OF GUINEA
Benue
ABUJA
NIGERIA
Kano
Zinder
Niger
Ogbomosho
Ibadan
Lagos
PORTO-NOVO
Niger Delta
BENIN
TOGO
GHANA
Lake Volta
ACCRA
LOME
Kumasi
IVORY COAST
YAMOUSSOUKRO
Abidjan
BURKINA FASO
OUAGADOUGOU
NIAMEY
MALI
Tombouctou
Ségou
BAMAKO
Senegal
SENEGAL
DAKAR
GAMBIA
BANJUL
BISSAU
GUINEA-BISSAU
Labé
GUINEA
CONAKRY
FREETOWN
SIERRA LEONE
MONROVIA
LIBERIA
NOUAKCHOTT
MAURITANIA
ATLANTIC OCEAN
Gambia
Senegal
Niger
DJIBOUTI
Dire Dawa
Nazret
Berbera
Hargeysa
SOMALIA
MOGADISHU
Marca
Kismayu
Jubba
Shabe
Webi
KENYA
UGANDA
Omo
GREAT RIFT VALLEY
INDIAN OCEAN
Awash

Did you know? The largest rough diamond was the 3106 carat Cullinan found in the Premier Mine, Pretoria, South Africa in 1905.

FACE THE FACTS...

❖ Land
High points in southern Africa are Mt Kilimanjaro in Tanzania (5895 m), Mt Kenya in Kenya (5199 m), and Mt Thabana-Ntlenyana in Lesotho (3482 m). The longest rivers are the Congo (4666 km) and the Zambezi (2700 km).

❖ Population
South Africa 42.1 m; Tanzania 32.9 m; Kenya 29.4; Uganda 21.4; Mozambique 17.3 m; Angola 12.3 m; Zimbabwe 11.9 m; Malawi 10.7 m; Zambia 9.8 m; Rwanda 8.3 m; Burundi 6.6 m; Lesotho 2.1 m; Namibia 1.7 m; Botswana 1.5 m; Swaziland 1 m; Equatorial Guinea 443,000.

❖ Capitals
See the map.

❖ Resources
Except for Angola, southern Africa is not rich in oil like the north. But it has an extraordinary wealth of metals such as copper, lead, tin, iron, uranium, platinum and gold, and of precious gems, notably diamonds. Namibia is the world's second-largest producer of lead, and has the world's biggest uranium mine. Angola, Namibia and South Africa are rich in diamonds. South Africa is the world's leading producer of gold, platinum, diamonds, chrome, manganese and vanadium.

❖ Agriculture
Much of the land in this part of the world is far too dry to farm intensively. Over most of the area, people grow food, typically maize, for themselves, or raise cattle. In the wetter places in East Africa, for example the Kenyan highlands, Zimbabwe and Mozambique, there are big plantations growing export crops such as tea, coffee, sugar, green beans and tobacco. South Africa, cooler and damper, grows a variety of crops.

❖ Industry
Outside South Africa, most of southern Africa is countryside, and industry is concentrated in a few major cities such as Bulawayo in Zimbabwe, where major products include steel, cement, cars, textiles, light machinery, processed food and cigarettes. In South Africa, industry is focused on Johannesburg and Pretoria and on ports – for example Durban.

❖ Government
European colonial rule left many southern African countries torn by tensions between tribal groups. Yet many countries are now multi-party democracies and South Africa has emerged since apartheid ended in 1994 as one of the most stable democratic countries in the region.

❖ Religion
Most people are either Christian or practise traditional beliefs.

❖ Language
Most people in southern Africa speak either English or one of the 100 or so Bantu languages, which include Zulu and Swahili.

❖ Sport
Athletics and cricket are popular.

Masai
The Masai are cattle herders who live on the southern borders of Kenya. They don't eat the cows, but milk them and drink small amounts of their blood by sucking it from a vein through a thin reed.

African tragedy
Burundi was once famous for its drummers who sent messages by beating huge drums, but in 1994 Burundi and neighbouring Rwanda became famous for something very different. They were savaged by the worst act of genocide in African history as tribal violence flared between the Tutsi and Hutu.

Mountains of the Moon
High in the misty, forested mountains of the Ruwenzori on the Uganda-Rwanda border is the last home of the mountain gorilla. This huge, gentle creature, the biggest of all primates, has been hunted almost to extinction and there are now very few left.

Trained copper
Zambia is the world's fourth-largest copper producer, and thousands of Zambians have moved to the mining towns of the copper belt because making a living by farming has become harder. Zambia relies on copper for 85 per cent of its exports.

Miles
0 100 200 300 400 500 600

Kilometres
0 100 200 300 400 500 600 700 800 900

INDIAN OCEAN

SOMALIA

ETHIOPIA

SUDAN

KENYA
NAIROBI
Mt. Kenya 5199m

UGANDA
KAMPALA
Lake Kyoga
Lake Albert
Lake Edward
Mt. Elgon 4321m
Kisumu
Mbale
Lake Victoria

Mwanza
Kilimanjaro 5895m
Mombasa
Tana
Equator

RWANDA
KIGALI
BURUNDI
BUJUMBURA
Lake Kivu

Pemba I.
Zanzibar I.
Mafia I.

TANZANIA
DODOMA
Tanga
Zanzibar
Dar es Salaam
Tabora
Rufiji
Rufuma

EASTERN RIFT VALLEY
GREAT RIFT VALLEY
WESTERN RIFT VALLEY
Lake Turkana
Lake Tanganyika
Lake Rukwa
Lake Nyasa

MADAGASCAR
ANTANANARIVO
Antsiranana
Tsaratanana 2876m
Mahajanga
Toamasina
Fianarantsoa

COMOROS
MORONI
MAYOTTE (to FRANCE)

Mozambique Channel

CONGO (DEMOCRATIC REPUBLIC)
KINSHASA
Kisangani
Mbuji-Mayi
Kolwezi
Lubumbashi
Congo
Uele
Lomela
Lomami
Lualaba
Kasaï
Lukenie
Kasaï
Lake Mai-Ndombe
Lubilash

CONGO BASIN

CONGO
BRAZZAVILLE
Pointe-Noire
Ubangi

GABON
LIBREVILLE
Port-Gentil

CAMEROON
MALABO
EQUATORIAL GUINEA
Bata
Bioko (to EQUATORIAL GUINEA)
GULF OF GUINEA

SÃO TOMÉ & PRÍNCIPE

Cabinda (to Angola)

ANGOLA
LUANDA
Lobito
Benguela
Lubango
Huambo
Kwango
Kwanza
Kasai
Cuito
Cunene
Okavango

MALAWI
LILONGWE
Blantyre
Lake Nyasa

MOZAMBIQUE
Beira
Nacala
Nampula
Zambezi
Save

ZAMBIA
LUSAKA
Kitwe
Ndola
Kabwe
Luangwa
Lake Bangweulu
Lake Mweru
Kafue
Zambezi

ZIMBABWE
HARARE
Mutare
Bulawayo
Victoria Falls
L. Kariba
Livingstone
Kariba Dam

BOTSWANA
Francistown
Selebi - Phikwe
KALAHARI

NAMIBIA
WINDHOEK
Swakopmund
Walvis
NAMIB DESERT
Okavango Basin
Rundu

ATLANTIC OCEAN

Messina
Lim...

Southern Africa

Much of southern Africa is a vast plateau – covered in the northwest by lush tropical forest, further south and east by grassy savannah and woodland and in the west and centre by the great Kalahari and Namib deserts. On the east of the plateau is the deep gorge of the Great Rift Valley, fringed by volcanoes such as Kilimanjaro. Most people still live in small hut villages, often with fewer than 50 inhabitants, and there are vast empty spaces occupied only by wildlife.

Victoria Falls, Zambia

The southern Africans

Southern Africa is home to hundreds of different black peoples, as well as small groups of Europeans and Asians. Some countries here are poor and deeply divided, like Rwanda. Many of the others, such as South Africa and Mozambique, are finally putting years of conflict behind them and building a more stable future.

Nelson Mandela
Until recently, South Africa was ruled by a tiny white minority, and black people were kept apart from whites by the unacceptable policy of apartheid. Nelson Mandela is the remarkable man whose leadership has helped bring apartheid to a peaceful end. For 26 years, Mandela was held in jail, despite protests from all round the world, for his role in the African National Congress (ANC), the organization fighting to end apartheid. When he was released in 1990, he at once took over the leadership of the ANC. From 1994 to 1999 he was South Africa's first black president.

Zambian tribal mask

Civil war
When the European colonial powers carved Africa up into nations, they ignored most of the different ethnic groups and lifestyles. All over Africa, national boundaries cut right across tribal lands, often leaving small isolated groups in countries dominated by different and often hostile tribes or cultures. This is one reason why so many African countries have been torn apart by civil wars, or been taken over by dictators.

Kanga and kikoy
Kikuyu women in Kenya often wear a rectangle of brightly coloured cotton called a kanga. Some men in Kenya wear a thick cotton wrap called a kikoy, which is like a long skirt.

Basic diet
Food is often very simple in Africa. For many people, the mainstay of the diet is ugali, a plain white dryish porridge made from pulverized corn.

More on top
People travel huge distances in southern Africa to get water, to sell things at markets and to buy things in town. Some will walk for hours or even days. Others cram on to the low-fare minibuses. These hurtle along, packed inside and out with people, their luggage and their animals.

Struggling to survive
Desperate poverty is all too common in southern Africa. In Mozambique, many children are reduced to picking up used cigarette ends from the street to save themselves from starvation – they collect the tobacco left behind and sell it for a pittance.

Round house
Square houses are quite new to Africa. In remote rural areas, some African people still live in traditional round huts made of poles, thatch and mud.

Elephants in the Serengeti game reserve, Tanzania

Big cat
Lions are the monarchs of the savannah. In the cool of the morning, they will lie in wait by waterholes for unsuspecting zebras and antelopes to drink, then pounce suddenly for a kill. Countries such as Kenya and Tanzania are known for their game reserves, which offer exciting encounters with lions and other big cats - and useful earnings from foreign tourists.

Gold diggers
Gold has helped to make South Africa the richest country in Africa. In the last 100 years, the gold mines at Witwatersrand near Johannesburg have produced nearly half the world's gold, and still produce almost a third of it every year. To dig out the gold, miners had to work in extremely hot, cramped, dangerous conditions.

Namibian uranium
Namibia doesn't only have the world's biggest uranium mine; it also has deposits of diamonds estimated at up to three billion carats. Not surprisingly, the country was coveted by neighbouring South Africa, and only achieved full independence in 1990 after a long campaign by the South West Africa People's Organization (SWAPO).

Did you know? In Swahili, minibuses are called *matatu*, or 'three more': even crammed full, there's always room for three more.

Did you know? The vast underground water reserves known as the Great Artesian Basin lie under nearly a fifth of the country.

Australia

Australia is huge, stretching across an entire continent from the Pacific to the Indian Ocean. Few other countries include such a wide variety of landscapes, from the rolling farmland of the southeast to the scorching desert interior.

FACE THE FACTS...

❖ Land
Australia's highest mountain is Mt Kosciusko (2228 m); its longest river is the Darling (2739 km).

❖ Climate
Australia is mostly very warm but it is so large that it includes a wide range of climates.

The north of the country is tropical, with temperatures in the hot, wet summers averaging more than 30°C; the southeast can be quite cool in winter, and July temperatures average 12°C.

❖ Population
18,967,000.

❖ Capital
Canberra.

❖ Resources
Australia has huge mineral resources, with vast reserves of iron, aluminium, zinc, gold and silver and coal.

❖ Farming
Most of the land is so dry that only 2 per cent of it is suitable for crops, although Australia is a major exporter of wheat. But two-thirds of the land is used for rearing sheep and cattle. Australian sheep produce almost a third of the world's wool.

❖ Forestry and fishing
The mountains of the southwest and Tasmania provide abundant wood, while coastal waters yield fish such as mullet, tuna and snoek.

❖ Industry and commerce
Manufacturing industry is growing in Australia, especially the production of cars and lorries, beer and electronic equipment.

❖ Government
Australia has its own parliament and prime minister. The British Queen (represented by the Governor-General) is actually the country's head of state but some Australians would prefer their own elected president instead. But the Queen is still popular with many Australians, despite Britain's location the other side of the world.

❖ Currency
Australians pay for things using the Australian dollar.

❖ Religion
The major religion is Christianity, but the Aborigines and other ethnic groups have their own religions.

❖ Sport
Sport is very popular in Australia, especially surfing, rugby, cricket and Australian rules football in which 18 players-a-side punch and kick a ball up and down an oval pitch.

The outback
Vast areas of Western Australia are empty and so flat, so remote that they are called the 'outback'. Sometimes Australians will 'go bush' and trek across the outback to escape from the stress of city life.

Alice Springs
The small town of Alice Springs is right in the centre of Australia, miles from anywhere on the edge of the vast Gibson desert. Huge dust storms whirl across the dry plains and engulf the town in dust at least ten times a year.

Australian jumper
Australia was cut off from the rest of the world many millions of years ago as the continents drifted apart. This means it has some unique animals. Best known is the kangaroo, a marsupial (the name given to animals which carry their young in a pouch).

All mine
Huge chunks of Australia are being dug out to extract the valuable metals in the ground. The Mt. Goldsworthy iron mine in Western Australia is thought to contain 15,000 million tonnes of ore.

The Great Reef
Stretching 1900 km along the north-eastern coast is the Great Barrier Reef, by far the largest coral reef. The beautiful coral and its teeming marine life are a magnet for divers and trippers in boats.

Koala
The cuddly koala is one of Australia's national symbols. But it feeds only on the leaves a certain type of eucalyptus tree. So many of these trees have now been cut down that the survival of the koala is seriously threatened.

Map labels

PACIFIC OCEAN

INDIAN OCEAN

PAPUA NEW GUINEA
SOLOMON ISLANDS
VANUATU
FIJI
NEW CALEDONIA
NEW ZEALAND
Coral Sea
Tasman Sea
AUSTRALIA
TASMANIA
ANTARCTICA

Port Hedland
Dampier
Fortescue
△ Mt. Bruce 1227m
Ashb...
Great Sandy Desert
Tropic of Capricorn

Darwin
Arnhem Land
Daly
Roper
Victoria
Kimberley Plateau
TIMOR SEA
ARAFURA SEA
Tanami Desert
NORTHERN TERRITORY
MACDONNELL RANGES
Alice
Barkly Tableland

Gulf of Carpentaria
Torres Strait
Cape York Peninsula
Cape York
Mitchell
Flinders
CORAL SEA
Great Barrier Reef
GREAT DIVIDING
QUEENSLAND
Cairns
Townsville
Lake Dalrymple
Mackay
Rockhampton

Flying doctor
In the interior, places are so far apart that many people get about by plane, including the doctor.

Sydney Opera House
The remarkable opera house in Sydney, modelled on a sailing ship, is one of Australia's best-known landmarks.

Ride the surf
With such a mild climate, it is hardly surprising that outdoor activities such as surfing (and windsurfing) are very popular in Australia. Christmas Day sees thousands of people head down to the famous Bondi Beach near Sydney for a beach party or to surf in the giant waves that roll in from the Pacific.

Windsurfer

Vineyards
Australia is becoming more and more famous for its wines from the vineyards of the southeast, especially the Hunter and Barossa Valleys. The grapes came originally from Europe, but they thrive in the mild climate.

Round up
The sheep flocks of the outback are far too big to be herded on foot, and many farmers ride around their farms on horseback or on motorbikes. On the biggest sheep stations, the farmer may even use an aeroplane to get around.

TASMAN SEA

Bass Strait

Sheep country
There are over 115 million sheep in Australia – more than in any other country in the world – and most of them are in New South Wales. Here vast farms called 'stations' cover thousands of kilometres.

and future. In celebrations of Dreamtime, the men decorate their bodies much as they do in the corroboree, described under Aborigine culture, left.

Digging for riches
The jewels and precious metals embedded in Australia's rocks have played a major part in the country's development, attracting thousands of prospectors to places such as the Kalgoorlie gold veins. Tourists can still go down to Coober Pedy and try their luck digging for opals with a pick and shovel.

Uluru
Rising out of the desert like a giant whale out of the sea, Uluru (Ayers Rock) is one of the world's oldest rocks. For the Aborigines it is sacred and the Australian government recently returned it to their care.

Mabo land on Murray Island occupied by his ancestors before the Europeans arrived.

Aborigine culture
Although 60 per cent of Aborigines now live in cities, they have their own unique culture and sense of identity and have their own distinctive celebrations and rituals, such as the corroboree, when Aborigine men decorate their bodies with white paint made from soil and crushed rocks.

Dreamtime
The idea of 'Dreamtime' is very important to the aborigines. Dreamtime is not only the dawn of all creation, when land, rivers, rain, wind and all living things were made, but also a thread linking the past, present

Long haul
Goods are often carried the vast distances across Australia in road trains. These are trucks that pull three or more trailers, called dogs, often at high speed.

Australians

For thousands of years, Australia's only inhabitants were nomadic tribes of hunters. The Europeans, who began to settle the country in the 18th century, called them Aborigines. Now the Aborigines make up only 1.5 per cent of the population. Most of the rest have European ancestors. Many recent immigrants are from Southeast Asia.

Aborigine rights
When the Europeans came, the Aborigines were driven from much of their land. Later they found themselves victims of prejudice, poverty and unemployment. To help compensate for the damage, the government is giving Aborigines special rights over places such as Uluru. A famous trial in 1992 returned Aborigine Eddie

Kilometres
0
100
200
300
400
500
600

Miles
0
100
200
300
400

Did you know? Children in some areas live so far apart that they attend Schools of the Air – they talk to the teacher by two-way radio.

Did you know? The Indian Pacific train travels from Perth to Sydney across the flat …

71

New Zealand

New Zealand was one of the last places to be inhabited by humans, and it is one of the least polluted countries in the world – a clean, beautiful land of rolling farmland, verdant forests and towering mountains. It is made up of two main islands – the almost subtropical North Island where most people live, and the long, narrow South Island, with its wide open Canterbury Plains and the soaring Southern Alps with their snowfields and glaciers.

FACE THE FACTS...

❖ The land
New Zealand's highest peak is Mt. Cook (3764 m), known in Maori as Aorangi, 'the cloud piercer'; the longest river is the Waitaki (425 km).

❖ Climate
New Zealand's climate is mild and often damp overall, but varies from the hot and rainy subtropical north to the cold of the southern mountains.

❖ Population
The population is just 3.8 m, in a country similar in size to the UK or Japan. Most people live on the North Island.

❖ Capital
The capital of New Zealand is Wellington, named after the famous British general, the Duke of Wellington.

❖ Natural resources
New Zealand has small reserves of natural gas, oil, coal and gold. But it has many fast-flowing rivers, which provide hydro-electric power, and volcanic heat sources beneath the ground which produce geothermal energy.

❖ Forestry
New Zealand has vast plantations of pine trees to provide timber, as well as native evergreens which are protected from exploitation.

❖ Farming
This is primarily an agricultural country, with over 50 per cent of the country devoted to crop and pasture. About 75 per cent of its exports are farm-based. Sheep and beef cattle are the main livestock. Key crops are maize and barley, plus fruit such as avocados, kiwi fruit and citrus fruits.

❖ Fishing
The waters around New Zealand are rich with fish such as barracuda, snapper, hoki and orange roughy. Oysters, mussels and other shellfish are farmed.

❖ Industry and commerce
Most of New Zealand's industry is based on processing farm, fish and forestry products. But other industries include steel, aluminium, textiles and electronics.

❖ Government
New Zealand is a parliamentary democracy. Essentially, it became independent from Britain in 1907, but the British Queen is still the head of government, represented by the Governor General.

❖ Religion
Most New Zealanders are Protestants, but the Maoris have their own religion.

❖ Currency
The New Zealand dollar.

❖ Sport
Rugby is the most popular sport.

Dairy fresh
New Zealand is famous for its dairy produce. Millions of cattle are reared on its lush green pasture. Farms are generally small, family-run affairs, typically just 120 cows on 5 hectares, but they are renowned for their efficiency, and New Zealand exports huge quantities of butter, cheese and milk.

Island paradises
Scattered across the western Pacific are thousands of beautiful volcanic and coral islands, covered with lush vegetation, including Fiji, Tonga and Western Samoa. In some places, the native islanders still live much as they always have, in their traditional houses roofed with fronds. But in others, a more Western lifestyle is taking over.

Kiwi fruit
Around the turn of the century, the Chinese gooseberry was brought here and planted in orchards. It thrived so well in the warm subtropical climate of the North Island that it was renamed the kiwi fruit after the New Zealand bird. Kiwi fruit are one of the country's major exports.

Buzz words
New Zealand is governed from the capital Wellington, called the Beehive because that is what it resembles. Among the 120 members sitting in the House of Representatives here, there are always at least five Maoris, elected exclusively by Maoris.

Gisborne
Poverty Bay

RAUKUMARA RANGE

Hawke Bay

Tauranga
Rotorua
Lake Waikaremoana

Napier
Hastings

△ *Ruapehu 2797m*

N O R T H   I S L A N D

Bay of Plenty

Waikato
Lake Taupo

Hamilton

Hauraki Gulf

Palmerston North

Great Barrier Island

Auckland

Wanganui

Wanganui

Whangerei

North Cape

THREE KINGS ISLANDS

New Plymouth
△ *Mount Egmont 2518m*

C o o...

Golden Bay
Tasman

T A...

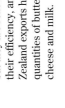

Kilometres / Miles

Scale: 0 50 100 150

PACIFIC OCEAN

SOLOMON ISLANDS
VANUATU FIJI **WESTERN SAMOA**
NEW CALEDONIA **TONGA**

NEW ZEALAND

Coral Sea

[PAPUA NEW GUINEA]

Tasman Sea

AUSTRALIA

TASMANIA

INDIAN OCEAN

ANTARCTICA

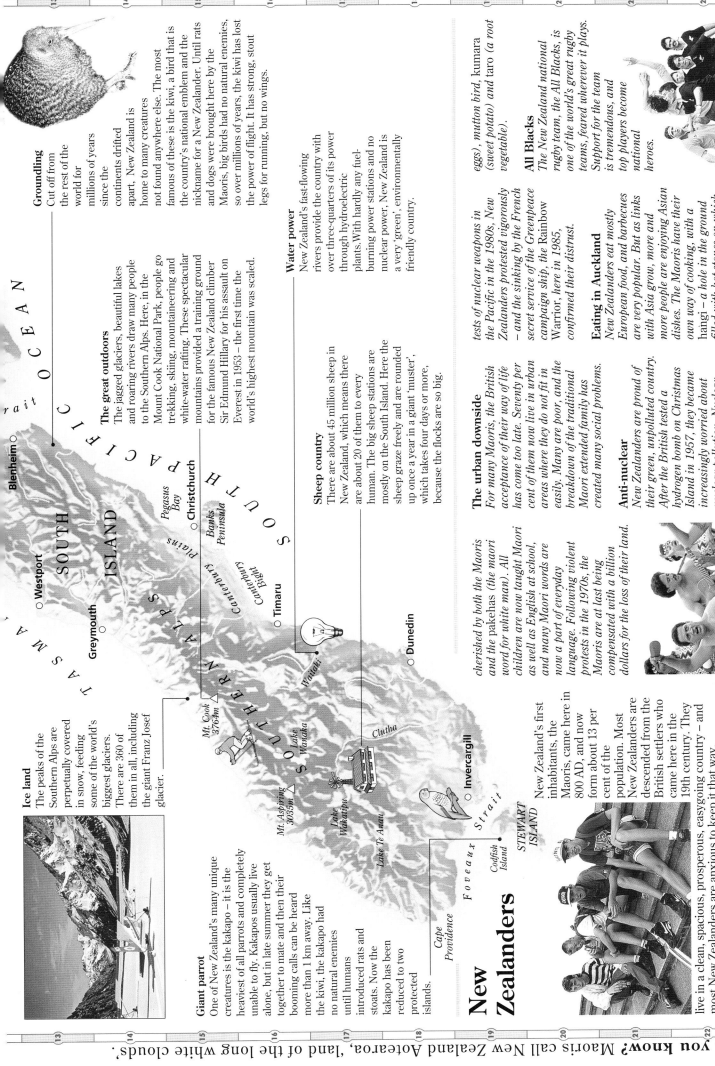

Grounding

Cut off from the rest of the world for millions of years since the continents drifted apart, New Zealand is home to many creatures not found anywhere else. The most famous of these is the kiwi, a bird that is the country's national emblem and the nickname for a New Zealander. Until rats and dogs were brought here by the Maoris, big birds had no natural enemies, so over millions of years, the kiwi has lost the power of flight. It has strong, stout legs for running, but no wings.

Ice land

The peaks of the Southern Alps are perpetually covered in snow, feeding some of the world's biggest glaciers. There are 360 of them in all, including the giant Franz Josef glacier.

Giant parrot

One of New Zealand's many unique creatures is the kakapo – it is the heaviest of all parrots and completely unable to fly. Kakapos usually live alone, but in late summer they get together to mate and then their booming calls can be heard more than 1 km away. Like the kiwi, the kakapo had no natural enemies until humans introduced rats and stoats. Now the kakapo has been reduced to two protected islands.

The great outdoors

The jagged glaciers, beautiful lakes and roaring rivers draw many people to the Southern Alps. Here, in Mount Cook National Park, people go trekking, skiing, mountaineering and white-water rafting. These spectacular mountains provided a training ground for the famous New Zealand climber Sir Edmund Hillary for his assault on Everest in 1953 – the first time the world's highest mountain was scaled.

Water power

New Zealand's fast-flowing rivers provide the country with over three-quarters of its power through hydroelectric plants. With hardly any fuel-burning power stations and no nuclear power, New Zealand is a very 'green', environmentally friendly country.

Sheep country

There are about 45 million sheep in New Zealand, which means there are about 20 of them to every human. The big sheep stations are mostly on the South Island. Here the sheep graze freely and are rounded up once a year in a giant 'muster', which takes four days or more, because the flocks are so big.

The urban downside

For many Maoris, the British acceptance of their way of life has come too late. Seventy per cent of them now live in urban areas where they do not fit in easily. Many are poor, and the breakdown of the traditional Maori extended family has created many social problems.

Anti-nuclear

New Zealanders are proud of their green, unpolluted country. After the British tested a hydrogen bomb on Christmas Island in 1957, they became increasingly worried about nuclear pollution. Nuclear power is now banned from the country entirely. Not even nuclear-powered ships are allowed to dock here. When the French began to resume

tests of nuclear weapons in the Pacific in the 1980s, New Zealanders protested vigorously – and the sinking by the French secret service of the Greenpeace campaign ship, the Rainbow Warrior, here in 1985, confirmed their distrust.

Eating in Auckland

New Zealanders eat mostly European food, and barbecues are very popular. But as links with Asia grow, more and more people are enjoying Asian dishes. The Maoris have their own way of cooking, with a hangi – a hole in the ground filled with hot stones on which the food is cooked wrapped in leaves (or nowadays,

eggs), mutton bird, kumara (sweet potato) and taro (a root vegetable).

All Blacks

The New Zealand national rugby team, the All Blacks, is one of the world's great rugby teams, feared wherever it plays. Support for the team is tremendous, and top players become national heroes.

New Zealanders

New Zealand's first inhabitants, the Maoris, came here in 800 AD, and now form about 13 per cent of the population. Most New Zealanders are descended from the British settlers who came here in the 19th century. They

cherished by both the Maoris and the pakehas (the maori word for white man). All children are now taught Maori as well as English at school, and many Maori words are now a part of everyday language. Following violent protests in the 1970s, the Maoris are at last being compensated with a billion dollars for the loss of their land.

live in a clean, spacious, prosperous, easygoing country – and most New Zealanders are anxious to keep it that way.

Maori pride

The Maoris lost their land after the British came and their way of life was severely damaged.

But although most Maoris now live Western lifestyles, the maoritanga – the Maori way of doing things – is increasingly

aluminium foil). They cook seafood such as eels and whitebait, as well as kina (sea

Map labels

- Blenheim
- Westport
- SOUTH ISLAND
- Greymouth
- Pegasus Bay
- Christchurch
- Banks Peninsula
- Canterbury Plains
- Canterbury Bight
- Timaru
- Dunedin
- Mt. Cook 3764m
- Mt. Aspiring 3035m
- SOUTHERN ALPS
- Lake Wanaka
- Lake Wakatipu
- Lake Te Anau
- Clutha
- Waitaki
- Invercargill
- STEWART ISLAND
- Codfish Island
- Cape Providence
- Foveaux Strait
- TASMAN SEA
- SOUTH PACIFIC OCEAN
- Strait (Cook Strait)

Did you know? Maoris call New Zealand Aotearoa, 'land of the long white clouds'.

73

Did you know? New Zealand was the first country to have a welfare state (in 1890) and the first to give women the vote, in 1893.

FACE THE FACTS...

❖ The land
The highest peak in the Arctic is Mt Gunnbjørn in Greenland (3700 m). There are few rivers in this frozen world. At the centre of it is the North Pole, surrounded by the permanently frozen Arctic Ocean – see below.

❖ Climate
It is cold all year round. During the long winter night when the sun never rises above the horizon, temperatures average –30°C and can drop as low as –70°C. During the brief summer, temperatures rise slightly above zero. The ice cap is technically a desert, since it is too cold ever to rain.

❖ Population
Various groups of people live within the Arctic Circle in Canada and Siberia. Greenland's population is 56,000; Svalbard's is 2,600.

❖ Wildlife
The tundra beyond the permanent ice supports a great deal of wildlife, including animals such as caribou, musk oxen, Arctic foxes and hares, wolves and lemmings, many insects and plants such as wildflowers and grasses.

❖ Resources
The Arctic contains a range of mineral resources including oil and gas on Spitsbergen, plus coal, uranium, gold, silver, copper, nickel, lead and zinc.

The Arctic

The Earth's north polar region is permanently covered with a vast, floating raft of ice up to 50 m thick – the polar ice cap. Beyond the ice are bleak, treeless islands and vast, low rocky landscapes blanketed in snow and ice for at least half the year.

Polar bears
Polar bears are the only big meat-eating mammals that live on the Arctic ice. Their main food is seals, which they catch by lying in wait at the seals' breathing holes. When a seal surfaces, the bear quickly swipes it with its paw then kills it with a swift bite to the head.

Ice coal
The world's most northerly coal mines are at Longyearbyen on the island of Spitsbergen. The island is cut off by ice for much of the year, so extracting the coal and shipping it elsewhere can be expensive.

Breaking the ice
Icebreakers play a vital role in the Arctic, not only breaking through to places that would otherwise become icebound, but keeping shipping lanes open, too. They are immensely powerful, strongly built ships, with reinforced steel bows cut away underneath so that the ship can slide up and over the ice and crack it by force of its weight.

Arctic ice
The ice covering the North Pole is called sea ice, because it floats on the ocean, but there are actually three kinds: polar ice, pack ice and fast ice. Most of the ice cap is polar ice, which is up to 50 m thick but melts in summer to as little as 2 m.

Fast ice
Fast ice forms in winter between the shore and the pack ice. It is called fast ice because it is held fast to the shore, so does not move up and down with the ocean as pack ice does.

Pack ice
Pack ice forms on the fringes of the polar ice. It is much thinner – only 2 m at most – and only freezes completely solid in winter. It is continually broken and crushed by the movement of the ocean, churning it into fantastic ice sculptures.

Map labels: RUSSIA · ARCTIC OCEAN · ALASKA · CANADA · GREENLAND · Nordvik · Kara Sea · Zemlya · Laptev Sea · Northern Land · Franz Josef Land · Barents Sea · New Siberian Islands · Ambarchik · East Siberian Sea · ARCTIC · Norwegian Sea · OCEAN · North Pole · Svalbard (to Norway) · Greenland Sea · Chukchi Sea · Bering Strait · Cape Lisburne · Point Hope · Lincoln Sea · Denmark Strait · ICELAND · Point Barrow · Barrow · ALASKA (to USA) · Beaufort Sea · Ellesmere Island · North Magnetic Pole · GREENLAND (to Denmark) · Mt. Gunnbjørn (3700m) · REYKJAVIK · M'Clure Strait · Banks Island · Queen Elizabeth Islands · Baffin Bay · ATLANTIC OCEAN · Cape Bathurst · Victoria Island · Davis Strait · Baffin Island · CANADA · GODTHÅB · Average permanent extent of sea ice

Scale: Kilometres / Miles — 0, 200, 400, 600, 800, 1000 / 0, 200, 400, 600, 800

FACE THE FACTS...

❖ The land
The highest peak in the Antarctic is the Vinson Massif (4896 m). There are no rivers in this frozen world. The South Pole lies more or less at the centre of this, the world's most southerly continent.

❖ Climate
The Antarctic is the coldest place on Earth. Temperatures rarely rise above zero and during the long winter they average –60°C. Technically it is a desert, since it is too cold ever to rain.

❖ Population
The population rises to 3000 in summer, but drops to 500 in winter when most researchers go home.

❖ Wildlife
The creatures that live here rely on the sea for food – there is only sparse moss and lichen on land. Seals and whales are the only mammals. Birds include a variety of penguins, plus, in summer, gulls and albatrosses.

❖ Resources
Antarctica has a rich range of mineral resources, but in 1991 nations agreed a ban on mining for 50 years to help keep the world's last wilderness unspoiled.

Emperor penguins
There are seven different kinds of penguin, all of which visit Antarctica from time to time. But only the largest of them, the Emperor penguin, braves the winter here.

Kilometres / Miles

ATLANTIC OCEAN
NORWEGIAN DEPENDENCY
South Georgia (to UK)
Average permanent extent of sea ice
INDIAN OCEAN
S. Orkney Is
ARGENTINE CLAIM
S. Shetland Is
AFRICA
ATLANTIC OCEAN
Weddell Sea
Halley (UK)
Coats Land
Queen Maud Land
Enderby Land
Mawson (Australia)
Drake Passage
Faraday (UK)
Antarctic Peninsula
BRITISH ANTARCTIC TERRITORY
Rothera (UK)
Palmer Land
Rønne Ice Shelf
AMERICAN HIGHLAND
Davis (Australia)
CHILEAN CLAIM
Bellingshausen Sea
Winson Massif 4896m
South Pole
GREATER ANTARCTICA
AUSTRALIAN ANTARCTIC TERRITORY
INDIAN OCEAN
LESSER ANTARCTICA
Amundsen-Scott (USA)
Mirnyy (Russia)
SOUTH AMERICA
ANTARCTIC
Byrd (USA)
Marie Byrd Land
Vostok (Russia)
Wilkes Land
Casey (Australia)
Amundsen Sea
Little America (USA)
Ross Ice Shelf
PACIFIC OCEAN
SOUTHERN OCEAN
AUSTRALIA
Russkaya (Russia)
Scott Base (NZ)
McMurdo Ross (USA) Sea
Victoria Land
Dumont d'Urville (France)
UNCLAIMED PACIFIC OCEAN
Leningradskaya (Russia)
South Magnetic Pole
FRENCH TERRITORY 'TERRE ADÉLIE'
ROSS DEPENDENCY (NEW ZEALAND)
AUSTRALIAN ANTARCTIC TERRITORY
TRANSANTARCTIC MOUNTAINS

Whale seas
The oceans around Antarctica are the summer home for all kinds of whales – blue whales, beluga whales, killer whales, white whales and humpback whales.

The Antarctic

Antarctica is a vast wilderness almost entirely covered by a layer of ice up to 4.5 km deep. It is the world's fifth largest continent, but it is cut off from the rest of the world by the cold and stormy Southern Ocean, and it is by far the coldest place on Earth.

Ice station
McMurdo is the largest of the American bases in Antarctica, with a population of up to 2000 in the summer. The other bases are the small Palmer Base, and the Amundsen-Scott, underground at the South Pole. The complex of research huts and accommodation at McMurdo is clustered round the hut Scott built on his 1902 expedition to the South Pole and includes a church, a post office, a cinema and a nuclear power station.

Polar people

Many different peoples live in the Arctic circle – the Lapps, Nenets, Yakuts and Chukchi in Eurasia, and the Inuit, Dene and Cree in North America and Greenland. Of these, the largest group is the Inuit of Greenland and northern Canada. Now many of them work in mines, on oil rigs and with the research scientists.

Keeping warm
To keep warm, people need at least three layers of clothing – including thermal underwear and an outer windproof and waterproof layer.

Good cores
The polar regions attract scientists for a variety of different research projects. Particularly valuable are 'ice cores'. The ice at the bottom of

the Antarctic and Greenland ice caps first fell as snow hundreds of thousands of years ago. By drilling into the ice and extracting cores of solid ice, scientists can obtain a remarkable record of the past.

The Inuit
The Inuit used to survive by hunting seals, caribou, walruses, polar bears and many other Arctic creatures, and they managed to stay healthy despite eating no fruit or vegetables whatsoever.

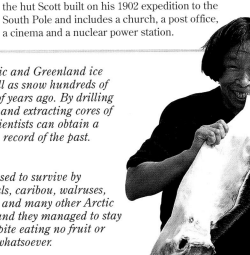

... bear, *Arctos*, because the Great Bear constellation is above the North Pole.

75

Index

Index

Photo credits

All pictures: Alligator Books Ltd except:–

Christine Osborne: MEP
p13 Oman:Wahiba Sands, p14 Sahel belt Ethiopia, p15 tea picker, paddy field worker (repeated on pp51 & 59), p27 cigar crop, p35 Tower Bridge, p37 café, p39 cheeses, p41 Red Cross building, p52 carpet, p53 Usbek couple, p55 United Arab Emirates boy, veiled woman, p58 Kuala Lumpur, hill tribe, p64 woman with bowl (repeated on p67), p66 pyramids and camels, p67 food, Moroccan women in traditional dress, p69 Victoria Falls, round hut, tribal mask, women, p71 truck, p73 boys.

John Noble: Wilderness Photographic Library
p13 Orsono volcano (repeated on p30), p29 Peruvian Indians, Machu Picchu, alpacas, p74 dog sleigh, p75 Inuit with sealskin, fisherman, penguins.

M. Wadlow: Russia and Eastern Images
p50 St Basil's Cathedral (repeated on p53).

Stephanie Colasanti:
p14 Mexican children (repeated on p26), woman selling rugs (repeated on pp17 & 29), p26 food picture, Mexican children, woman with basket, p27 Panama Canal, p63 geisha girl, children.

Jerome Snyjder:
p36 TGV, p37 Parisian girls, wine, p38 Amsterdam, p39 tulips, restaurant, windmill, p42 old man, p43 girl, fish, p45 girl on moped, p57 boy, p58 jeepney, p59 Thai girl, p61 Guilin, panda, dancers, p71 Aborigine, windsurfer, wine, Ayers Rock.

Neil Setchfield:
p31 young couple, musician, tango dancers, p35 businessman, Protestant marcher, Notting Hill Carnival, p47 young couple.

New Zealand Tourist Board: p73 All Jacks, Maoris, Tasman glacier, kiwi.

Thai Tourist Authority: p14 Thai boats.

Austrian National Tourist Office: p32 snowboarder (repeated on p41), p41 girl.

Swiss National Tourist Office: p41 snowman.

Finnish Tourist Board: p43 sauna.

SIS (Stockholm Information Service): p43 skater.

Government of India Tourist Office: p56 tiger, p57 elephant, Sikh.

Paul Ratigan: p60 Great Wall, p61 Chinese woman.

Japan National Tourist Organization: p63 sushi, seated eaters.

Mountain High Maps® Copyright © 1993 Digital Wisdom, Inc.